You can have, be, ~~only thing stopping~~ ~~and feelings which you are~~ these, and you remove the blocks to your accomplishing whatever you wish in life. Remove these, and you will find love, happiness, and joy beyond your wildest dreams. Remove these, and you are Free.

Lester Levenson

This book is for your heart... In this book Yuri makes you ask yourself... Can I learn to trust something more than my own mind? Like Alice in Wonderland and her steps through the mirror am I really so close and still not seeing: 'IT' has been within me all the time? Why do I insist on hanging on to my mind's guidance when it really knows so little about Life, the Universe and all that it contains? Can I quiet my mind long enough to give my heart the first say in the rest of my life's journey? I have found this to be a priceless exercise. And I am now embracing this journey that I have always been on but for the first time with an embracing of no limits to the volume of love I can contain. I've turned the mirror around and I see my inner self

Jill Sloan, Kernville, CA

I want to tell you that Freedom Technique really works. It takes some effort but it's worth it. Things started happening to me — things I wanted but was afraid of and thought impossible to happen. It was something I wished for during the whole summer. And it came without any work on my part. It just came. And I was able to take advantage of every moment without thinking of the past or future. Really, it was so exiting to see how things came together in a perfect manner. It's like suddenly I was able to complete the hardest puzzle.

Polina, Moscow, Russia

For me the best thing about Freedom Technique was the discovery of certain very real, concrete and key psychological methods, the practice of which can only but lead to increased awareness, love and to result in healing, success, and enlightenment. These methods take a very balanced and gentle approach, helping to calm and work with feelings we would rather run away from. In doing so, one learns to become one's own full-time psychologist, an enormous growth step for almost everyone. With proper practice, it can lead to the emergence of the ideal inner parent who binds up the wounds and dresses the scars of our not-so-easy lives.

But the book has more than just psychotherapeutic value. Much care and attention is devoted to placing the Freedom Technique method into the center of an entire religious world view. This holistic approach leads the reader beyond just himself and his problems and beyond the questions, hurts, and limitations which mere psychology could never answer, heal, or transcend.

By offering a horizon of utter fulfillment, Freedom Technique strengthens and gives courage to readers to start on the path of awareness and love critical to healing, success, and wholeness.

Thomas Finnell, Ohio

Dedicated to the Memory of

LESTER LEVENSON

"An American Saint"
and

OSHO

"An Unusual Saint"

ALSO BY YURI SPILNY

Gates of the Dead

The Incredible Adventures of Kitto:

Sorceress' Spell

The Toynapers

River of Fire

Freedom Technique

Published in Russia

Based on True Events

Book One

FREEDOM TECHNIQUE

Path to Awareness and Love

with

Autobiography of Lester Levenson

Yuri Spilny

BOOKSTOENJOY

A DIVISION OF LOVEANDWISDOM PUBLISHERS

BooksToEnjoy.com
Yuri's Hill
Peppermint Meadow, HC1, Box 106
Kernville, CA 93238

Copyright © 2011 by Yuri Spilny

For information about the book, please write to
yuri@bookstoenjoy.com

Order books: www.createspace.com/3694994

Editors Jill Sloan and Herb Neu

Translated, in part, from Russian by Thomas Finnell

Library of Congress © TXu-1-742-711

ISBN ISBN-13: 978-1466367975; ISBN-10: 1466367970

Contents

Rise, awaken, seek the wise and realize. The path is difficult to cross like the sharpened edge of the razor, so say the wise.

Verse 1.3.14 from the Katha Upanishads

Introduction

You can have, be, and do whatever you will or desire. The only thing stopping you is the accumulation of negative thoughts and feelings which you are subconsciously holding. Remove these, and you remove the blocks to your accomplishing whatever you wish in life.

Remove these, and you will find love, happiness, and joy beyond your wildest dreams.

Remove these, and you are Free.

These few lines express the essence of Lester Levenson's Releasing method that he proved with his life. The last chapter of this book is devoted to the Autobiography by Lester that I have illustrated with pictures. I placed Lester's memoir in the end because it doesn't describe the techniques and I believe that understanding the techniques will help the reader to better identify with Lester's message, whose meaning is often hidden between the lines. Yet another reason is that in his Autobiography, Lester, time and time again hints to the utmost importance of Love, which is also the subject of *Freedom Technique: Path to Awareness and Love, Book Two*[1].

The purpose of both books is to help in learning the reasons behind our choices, which will contribute to a better understanding and a more effective removal of the blocks. It provides tools that enable one to make the right decisions, achieve goals, and when ready, to choose Freedom.

Sooner or later each of us has to choose between freedom and slavery.

It may sound surprising, but the majority of us prefer slavery. Even more surprising is that we believe it is normal to be a slave. Of course the word "slave" is never used. Nevertheless, many of us are slaves, especially in this, our money driven society.

One may be the wealthiest person in the world or a penniless beggar; still both, most likely, are slaves. One is slave to possessions, concepts and passions; the other is slave to poverty, concepts and passions. No outside force makes one wealthy or poor, happy or miserable, wasting one's life in slavery or striving to be free. We do it—and for the most part we create these states unconsciously—all of them, except Freedom.

Fortunately, *Awareness* and *Freedom* are in our nature. In order to be free we need to become aware of our nature.

A free person can choose and live in the way he knows is the most appropriate. A slave believes in something outside himself as giving him wealth or punishing him as a beggar. One who walks the road of Freedom fulfills his own destiny.

---

[1] *Book Two* will be available in 2012 in paperback as well as in e-book format.

Human being is Awareness and has a body and a mind.

Those who know this are striving to be aware at all times. They release the spell of negative thoughts and emotions' influence, and realize the importance of accepting full responsibility for their lives and understand the meaning of *having no resistance, no fear and no wants*[2].

The Mind that is beyond an emotional-thinking process and beyond subconscious is a Pure Mind or Pure Awareness[3]. Pure Mind knows of its creative nature, but it doesn't create. In order to create, a free one must 'lower' himself to the world of illusion. Only in the world of thought, Mind will be able to exercise its creative ability. However, in the realm of thought the mind already is not pure, it is 'contaminated' by thought (and ego).

However, the difference between creative ability of the free one and that one of an average person is still in purity of the mind. When free one 'lowers' himself to the realm of thought, he is still beyond influence of the subconscious, he doesn't think, but employs only one thought that is necessary to create what is needed. Because it is unobstructed, this thought becomes extremely concentrated

---

[2] Paradox of Wanting is explained in *Nature of Want, Resistance, Fear and Releasing.*

[3] Pure Awareness is Pure Mind, our essence, Self, which is not limited by concepts, ideas and emotions, which has no subconscious mind. We call it Mind (with a capital 'A'). Pure Mind is never limited. Concepts, ideas and emotions that are superimposed over the Mind, create illusion of limitation. To this illusion of limitation humanity gave name of the mind (with small 'm'). In this book we also call it mind (small 'm'), in order to distinguish it from the unlimited Mind or Awareness.

and thus highly potent, allowing for almost instant materialization of what is being created.

As a result of some causes, I began my search for Truth many years ago. The teachings of the masters, years of meditation and that precious time, which I spent with Lester Levenson and Larry Crane[4], caused me to rethink my life. Releasing, taught by Lester, enabled me to change my life the way I wanted, transforming it into a beautiful journey.

Releasing is an important ingredient of this work.

This book is called *Freedom Technique*, because being a practical manual it demonstrates tools rooted in universal wisdom, which may help anyone willing to leave behind all chains of slavery, live a happy life and become free. Based on experience, I have included in this work a number of essential topics expounded upon by the teachers of the past, in support of the inner state of *Awareness, Love and Responsibility*—the three whales of Freedom Technique.

In order to re-discover these states of *Awareness, Love and Responsibility*, it is necessary to walk a path of *Releasing*, which is a path of *No Fear, No Resistance and No Wants.*

Freedom Technique will help you to fulfill your destiny; not the destiny your mind makes you believe is yours, but the destiny you have been born to fulfill. Thus, you will have a life of happiness, of peace, and a life of harmony of your inner and outer being.

As you practice, you will learn that your past will no longer influence you. Your regrets of the past and fears of the future will leave forever and from moment to moment you will be always in the present, loving ever more and experiencing life of fulfillment.

---

[4] www.releasetechnique.com Lessons, Seminars, Free weekly teleconferences

You will use the techniques to accomplish goals, to live your dreams and realize while in the process that you are the master of your life, that everything is possible and completely made available to you. As a result of this experience, an unshakable confidence will become forever yours, thus convincing you that indeed you have an inborn ability to sail the ship of your life to a destination of your choice and to Freedom – the most desirable destination of all.

For those who trust themselves, who believe in no boundaries, who strive to find Truth, may *Freedom Technique* become a loyal partner on the way to happiness and Freedom.

From the Author

Ah, moon of my delight, who knows no wane.
The Moon of Heaven is rising once again:
How often hereafter rising shall she look
Through the same garden after me – in vain!

Omar Khayyam in The Rubaiyat[5]

Awakening is an unusual state. At the same time this state is very natural to every human being. It is a purely personal experience beyond any comprehension of the mind and beyond words.

---

[5] Omar Khayyam poems are translated by Edward Fitzgerald unless noted otherwise.

The day before my birthday I wrote to my friend Alexander:

"Today is a sad day, because tomorrow is my birthday and it seems I am as far from Freedom as I was years ago, when I have made my first step on the path. Many years flew by, came and were gone unusual experiences, echoes of spiritual voices, revelations and intellectual understanding of the masters, a breeze of Freedom…"

Through the window are snow-capped mountains of the Sierra Nevada Range looming larger and Blue Jays are dancing around manger.

Winter.

Knowing that waiting is pointless, somewhere deep in my heart a flame of faith and love is dancing: spring comes when it comes…"

My birthday was probably the most difficult day ever. Outside, huge snowflakes whirled down slowly and it looked like the sun left gloomy skies forever.

Early in the morning, emotions assaulted me without mercy. I did not experience such a vicious attack since a very long time ago. As a matter of fact, I was convinced there was almost no negativity left within…. The assault continued all day long and into the night…

Determined, I kept welcoming assaulting emotions, immediately letting them go, using releasing, which by this time has become a second nature to me — a natural part of me. But there was something very unusual about this fierce emotional flood. This thought several times surfaced in my mind, but its real meaning I came to understand only on the morning of the following day.

It was a peaceful morning, very peaceful indeed… A large bird flew outside. With my eyes, I followed its flight and suddenly froze, enchanted with a panorama opening before me.

Mountains stood still as if waiting for something unusual to happen. I felt very peaceful. There were no thoughts either, just emptiness filled with solemnity of incredible sight before me. Every morning I have admired this majestic, ever changing view from my bedroom window, but today it was something extraordinary. Another moment and, suddenly, I realized that something extraordinary is happening to me.

The window vanished. I also vanished. There was only a sense of oneness with the mountains, with whole world, with the universe; there was no single thought, everything, including me just was just lived. Nothing seemed to change, but I ceased to exist along with all teachings, revelations, or spiritual experience. Such a wonderful "I, the seeker" was gone.

As usual, I brewed a cup of berry tea, then walked out to the deck and fed the birds. My body moved naturally and some thoughts flew by then disappeared, but all this was happening in a somewhat strange, unusual manner, seeming much lighter. My body felt lighter and thoughts did not cause me any reaction to them; they were appearing from nowhere and disappearing into nothingness. Everything, including any memory was left behind. I was beyond my mind, in some other dimension and in here at the same time. An incredibly deep, almost palpable peace settled in and all around me. Everything, including myself, was still, frozen, and then disappeared into peace. Only Awareness was left and sense of some truly unusual happening.

"Is it really that simple?" a thought crossed my mind. At the same time I realized that it was a useless question. I happened to be at home, where everything is natural, simple, comfortable. And this home was the entire world, everything that exists and beyond. I did not know what was "beyond", but this "something" was as natural to me as everything else.

That day I wrote in my diary: "Happy Birthday. Today I am born!"

Many strange — inexplicable at the time — happenings took place in my early life, related to Freedom. Some of them are mentioned throughout this book, exemplifying steps leading to Freedom.

My life has been an incredible adventure, a miracle. Even while in totalitarian Russia, I was often able to do what I chose. My panorama included the Naval Academy, the Moscow Film School, the Sakhalin Islands. As a boy, I wanted to travel around the world, which was an impossibility for the average young person living in the USSR. Yet, my earlier visions became my reality.

For years I traveled the globe while writing and producing documentary films. My life seemed effortless. Not one the wisdom of *The Taoist I Ching* warned me of about those who are not free, think they are fulfilled, when in fact they are empty. Self-satisfied, though reverent outwardly, they are not respectful inwardly; diligent in the beginning, they end up lazy... But I was ignorant and did not heed the warning.

Unknown to me, the then-causes of my good luck were exhausted. I start experiencing negativity—apathy, grief, fear; all that we so wisely call 'being human'. I began to sink. Still, I was able to do things, but every action required much effort. A state of despair became my sad companion...

But remembering how good my life had been, I started a search for the lost formula of success that in past years enabled me to accomplish my wishes. I wanted only success, yet my search inexplicably put me on the road of Freedom. I have studied the teachings of the masters and practiced long hours of meditation, where I experienced glimpses of pure Awareness. It was not until after I've met Lester Levenson and years of practice of releasing that I had the experience described in the beginning of this chapter.

The World

> With them the seed of wisdom did I sow,
> And with my own hand labored it to grow;
> And this was all the harvest that I reaped –
> "I came like water, and like wind I go."

Due to the causes created by ourselves unknowingly, we all appear to be different on the surface of life—a wonderful diversity, an incredible tapestry made of six billion illusory actors, playing their roles on the stage called earth. But the "tapestry" unites us; an appearance of diversity is oneness in reality. A collective consciousness is made of six billion individual consciousnesses as one; this collective consciousness makes this world the way it is today. There is no force that can implement an everlasting change of the collective consciousness except its natural evolution. And there is no force that could ever change collective consciousness, but awareness and Love[6] will.

Throughout history, powerful leaders tried to alter peoples' mentality achieving only a temporary result: their every attempt to force such change has eventually ended in disaster. However, a leader cannot really be

---

[6] Love with a capital 'L' here means true Love, which is wholly accepting and totally selfless, as opposite to what people are usually mean by love (with a small 'l').

17

blamed for what he does, as he is a natural product of the nation's collective consciousness, driven by emotions... Thusly America "produced" Thomas Jefferson; Cuba, Castro; France, Napoleon; and Russia produced Lenin.

When a baby is born, from day one it is subtly influenced by the collective consciousness of a nation and the world, as well as by parents, teachers and the society. The child is rarely led to discover that he is born to succeed. Instead, from the early childhood we are taught how to be slaves surviving in a life of sorrow. You need to rediscover your natural powers and build your life the way you wish it to be; it will lead you back home to peace, Love and harmony.

To start with, it is helpful to develop the ability to persevere, which means to continue in face of obstacles, pain, fatigue, frustration, opposition or hardship. To persevere is to continue to the end. Perseverance is a quality that enables us not to be worn down by anything. With perseverance the techniques will enable you bear any condition, overcome any obstacle and reach goals.

There is so much suffering in this world. Hundreds of millions of us eke out a meager existence, and those who have it all, still cannot find fulfillment. In this truly splendid world human life seems woven from a senseless series of events, ending in nothingness, only blue screens and billboards eternally shine here with smiles of happiness.

> This all a chessboard of nights and days
> Where destiny with men for pieces plays:
> Here and there moves and mates and slays,
> And one by one back in the closet lays.

The world we live in is beautiful, but in a strange human world millions die in wars, not having understood what they lived for, and millions are condemned to suffer a life of hunger and misery. Death here plucks out flowering life, and the ruler is greed and lies. Human life seems like nothing but a fleeting moment. Everything in it comes in for an instant and disappears without a trace, forever.

Shadowy hopes of happiness often end in disappointment, affording only now-and-then a temporary fulfillment. But the occasional success entices us to persuade it again and again; we are always hoping that the next goal we will surely reach and another relationship will be forever happy. Like any other experience, sooner or later every success must come to an end, because this cycle is the very nature of all experience. We need to learn how to be happy independently of success or failure, in any circumstance.

Only right knowledge is power. Once we learn it, we will know the rules and will play the game called life as Masters; we will enjoy our natural state of calm confidence and achieve independence of circumstances. A horrible world is an illusion, created by us unknowingly. In reality this world is a world of splendid beauty and harmony. All we need to do to experience it is to wake up to its Love, harmony and oneness.

Omar Khayyam lived in Persia over a thousand years ago. He had a very unusual life and he left this world a free man. In his deeply symbolic verses which are presented through out this narrative he often hints that it is useless to put oneself in the dependence of things, people, anything. We already have all we need to lead happy lives.

Ah, Love! Could thou and I with Fate conspire
To grasp the sorry Scheme of Things entire,
Would not we shatter it to bits – and then
Re-mould it nearer to the Heart Desire!

19

By understanding the importance of inner laws of Awareness, Responsibility and Love and freeing oneself of the influence of negative thoughts and emotions, anyone will be able to re-mould life to one's heart's desire.

Wealth helps, but alone it can not make us happy. True fulfillment can only be attained in a balanced existence, where material pursuits go hand in hand with inner peace.

How contradictory our life is! Now this world is horrible, now it is splendid, now it is loving, now it is hateful... When we are in love, wars, anger, greed all disappear, and a paradise of love blooms all around us, but a moment later our love is gone, the spring is gone and a world is back on our shoulders with all its heaviness.

Most people do not believe that happiness is possible. They forever damn themselves to suffering in slavery of desperate life of the struggling with obstacles of their own making. However, every human being is born free and has everything in himself, necessary for realization of his inborn happiness.

It seems we all know what life is, what love is, how to be happy. Why then do we have so much disappointment, so much pain? Maybe it is because others are causing our suffering, our failures? Or is it we who are ultimately responsible for everything that happens in our lives?

Once we know the how, it is then possible to rediscover our inborn ability to make ourselves naturally independent of circumstances, of others' approval, and know, at the same time, that all people and all things are connected, that the world is One. Still amidst people and circumstances, they will no longer influence us.

Today, our world is full of contradictions. The Creator exists for some and does not exist for others. Maybe the world is eternal and without a Creator, and there was never a beginning or an end? We don't know, but we make assumptions. Lack of right knowledge, desperate want of control, as well as of approval from others, binds us with chains of *want*, *resistance*, and *fear*, which is in perfect accord with universal law of compensation. *Resistance* renders us blind to opportunities, *fear* paralyzes us and attracts what we fear[7], and *want* is lack that creates dependence. We are very rarely confident in ourselves, most of us are afraid of the future. Information that we are receiving is always someone's word. But can we really trust anything that is not our own experience?

Only personal experience can give true understanding. But even this is not available to us until we begin to release our negativity, much of which was given to us by parents, society, school, friends, religion... Somewhere in the past all these negative concepts have been accepted by our parents, grandparents, and on and on, back to time immemorial. Down the line we will learn to let go of all concepts, for any concept is a limitation, obscuring Awareness.

Many religions exist in the world. They teach of the importance to be loving and compassionate, to be one with God, with the world and universe, how to meditate and to chant mantras, promising that in exchange we will receive an ultimate gift of eternal paradise. However, most of these teachings will not provide us with an effective method that is easy to implement.

The masters were teaching truths for millenniums. For Truth never changes. Lao Tzu and Buddha, Huang Po and

---

[7] When we are persistently fearful of something, we keep that 'something' in our mind. Mind is creative. What we doggedly keep in mind may materialize, sooner or later.

21

Bodhidharma, Rumi and Omar Khayyam, Paramahanza Yogananda, Jesus, Sai Baba and Lester Levenson utilized the same truths in their teachings of happiness. However, the teachings of the masters are often difficult to comprehend because of its symbolic language. *Freedom Technique* has these truths at its core, but the presentation is one of a practical guide which is easy to use in daily life. The techniques may be applied at any time while doing your work, driving, cooking or watching television. The more disturbing the circumstances, the more appropriate it is to practice these techniques.

***

Everyone wants to live a happy life. Unfortunately, we are too often making our happiness dependent on something, which can never give us lasting happiness: people, things and the world. We satisfy ourselves with crumbs of happiness and do not believe that happiness can be obtained in full measure. In our lethargic state, most of us cannot even imagine life without suffering. We do not govern our life; our mind and body govern it.

The meaning of the word "mind" (human or conscious mind) is deceiving. When we say "mind", it appears as if there is something within us. There is nothing! The mind is not a thing: it is a process of thinking, comparing and computing. Mind is a survival device. It is necessary to have in order to live in society. This mind, this process of thinking, is just a fragment of our Mind, and this fragment is trying to be independent and dominating. But it is impossible for a fragment to dominate; it creates conflict. Being a limitation, the fragment is failing all the time. That is why there is so much frustration in life. You, the mystery,

22

are bigger and incomparably more powerful. The mind is just a fragment but you gave it control.

It is the same with ego or our 'i'. Where can it be found? Nowhere. Ego or 'i' is just another thought in a stream of the thought process, and can be found nowhere. Continue our search even further, we will realize there is no real 'i' that is thinking; there is only a spontaneous thought process that is triggered by either an external world or by our subconscious and by demands of our body. If you are still convinced that you are a thinker, then tell me what is going to be your following thought? You will quickly realize it is an impossible task. Then, who is thinking? You will find no thinker. Thus there is no ego and no personality, no actor playing his funny or tragic role on the stage called Earth. All of these are symbols created by our mind in order to sustain relationships, as well as for convenience of communication.

However, the mind is creative; it is a root from which all things grow in our life. It is like a root of the tree, which is entirely dependent on it. Everything 'good' and 'bad' comes from our mind. To find something beyond the mind is impossible; there is nothing else but Mind or Awareness. The mind is the only creator. In the course of practice you will come to a better understanding of your mind, make it your true server and find your life dramatically changing for the better. The more you are released, the closer you are to your home, and the more you will take charge of your life, and greater will be your material progress. This is why it is said: after acquiring inward treasures, you will find that an outward supply is always forthcoming in abundance.

Everything material is rooted in the spiritual, both being one. Your success will no longer depend on "luck" or forgotten cause of the past, which turns into despair with the cause being exhausted. Instead, it will depend entirely on your conscious decision and responsible following through, for you will be always aware of who you are—a creator—living mystery.

Until we wake up, our life is but an endless struggle with the world and ourselves, which we proudly call something like "overcoming difficulties of life", "maturing", "enduring" or "growing". Life smiles at us, but very rarely. We believe that life smiles more often to others, but this is just another illusion, because the others only appear to be looking happier.

We are united by a general trait: we all want to be happy, but very few of us are looking for happiness where it actually is, and as a result, become happier. Others are looking for it in people, in the world, where it cannot be found.

Happiness can be found only within. This is our inherent quality. It is freedom from any dependence—and before all—dependence from the limitations we superimposed upon our mind and emotions.

Forever truly happy can be only one who is free, who is not dependent on anything whatsoever and therefore calm and peaceful in any situation. This also means acquiring an ability of letting go of negative thoughts and emotions even before they fully surfaced in our mind. To be free from thoughts and emotions does not mean suppressing them. Simply one becomes independent of the thought process' influence, peacefully observing the appearance and disappearance of thoughts and emotions, without being affected by them.

Thus Freedom means harmony with ourselves and the universe, having no *Resistance*, no *Fear* and no *Wants*. Having no resistance to all that is, is acceptance. This is oneness with all existence. We cannot make exceptions here, because not accepting even a single blade of grass means rejecting a part of ourselves and destroying oneness with illusion of partiality. Oneness is independence. It is not knowledge of every detail in the universe, but acceptance and readiness to be aware of everything in the universe and beyond, including all ideas and concepts of humanity. Dependence or attachment sprouts from fragmentation and fear of losing that little fragment of creation, which you imagine owning, or not receiving what is desired. When in our consciousness we are the universe, how can anything be lost? Fear is a result of separation and is the most dangerous advisor. Thus any dependence, be it a person, an object, or a situation, creates a conflict between our inborn state of oneness and Freedom and a condition of dependence. Any relationship that is based on dependence ends in ruin, as a rule.

Freud and Nietzsche affirmed that happiness was not possible. But people are not interested in others' opinion when it comes to happiness; everyone in his own way they continue to seek it out. Freud and Nietzsche were philosophers. Happiness is reality, and not at all a philosophy, which is always superficial. Philosophers and preachers will waste many words, telling you about happiness, about Freedom, but they are not able to show you what is needed to be done in order to become happy. This is why there are so many preachers and philosophers, but there is no happiness.

A bird builds a nest without knowledge, not having any philosophy, and no idea about nests. No one taught it how to do it. It is the bird's natural condition. Freedom and happiness are our natural condition. Deep within we know they exist. In reality, every person can be free now, but only when the decision to find freedom will be sincere and first in priority.

In order to realize this state of being, you have to learn to manage your mind, to make it calm, and then, to become independent from its limitations or transcend the limitations. This is the only way to become free.

Through thinking, the mind tries to compare, relate, and in this way to explain things. When one is free and knows all he needs to know for continual growth, there is no need for a cognitive relationship to things. We intuitively know all that is necessary to know in each given moment. That's why we are free—free from the limitations of concepts, dependencies and doubts. At the same time we always retain the ability to use our mind when it is necessary for communication with the world.

Feelings don't disappear when one becomes free. The difference between an ordinary person and the one, who is free, is that the former is subject to his mind, emotions, circumstances, whereas the decisions and actions of the latter are spontaneous and entirely independent from these three factors.

A free person lives in the present; the past cannot affect any influence upon him/her. It is more appropriate to say that free people live beyond time, in the Eternal Now—a dimension, meaning of which is for an ordinary perception will be more like "in the present".

Physicists as well as enlightened masters maintain that time is not an absolute reality. Einstein's work proves that space and time, which use to be separate and absolute, are actually intertwined and relative. In massive gravitational fields of black holes, for example, time slows down or even come to a full stop.

Shortly before his death in 1955, Einstein wrote: "For us believing physicists, the distinction between past, present and future is only an illusion even if a stubborn one." Time is man made concept that doesn't govern the universe, but it has great influence upon humanity. An ordinary person cannot overcome this influence; a free one can.

Thusly, the free one is beyond division of past, present and future. There is a higher awareness and consciousness of the eternal Now. As a result of deeper realization he may even become aware of all happenings before the time of Abraham, all happenings after him, and all happenings yet to come throughout eternity. This brings us closer to a mystery of prophecy and the law of compensation, of cause and effect.

Usually people are never in the present; they either live in memories of the past, or worry about the future. Balancing between past and future, they are seemingly at peace only in front of a television screen or when asleep. But even there, they are not at peace, since both in sleep, and in front of the idiot box, the mind continues its "underground" activity. A free person can simply "turn" his dreams on and off as if by order, and the same way he can change his destiny as if by magic.

The lives of ordinary people are predetermined. Their internal "computer"—subconscious mind—is programmed.

The moving finger writes: and having writ,
Moves on: no all thy piety nor wit
Shall lure it back to cancel half a line,
No all thy tears wash out a word of it.

Belief System or subconscious is a *moving finger* that *writes* our program of destiny in accordance with the law of cause and effect. Neither the religious approach of piety, nor the ways of sorrow or human intelligence will change our program of destiny.

We cannot change subconscious programs, until we begin practicing releasing. You will begin making conscious changes when you learn to keep in your mind only what you wish to see in your life, when your mind becomes your servant.

Our nature is pregnant with a spectrum of limitless possibilities for realization of our dreams. Would it not be logical to explore these possibilities, utilize them, and obtain happiness? However, it is first necessary to decide that we do not wish to be just another sheep in this huge flock which calls itself society and that we really do want to be truly happy.

Fate exists. Life is predestined, but only for those who live by the law of the crowd, with its artificial rules. Such an existence goes on and on until you liberate yourself and become forever free.

Lester Levenson on Happiness and Freedom[8]

> And that inverted bowl we call the sky,
> Where under crawling coop't we live and die,
> Lift not thy hands to it for help—for it
> Rolls impatiently on us thou and I.

That afternoon, he went home to his penthouse as though to a tomb. "It is a tomb," he thought, "and I'm a dead man. I guess I'll just have to get used to it." His sisters wanted to help and offered to take turns staying with him, to take care of him, but he sent them away. He just wanted to be by himself.

He went to bed and mostly slept for three days, waking up only occasionally to eat, or take his medicines, or use the bathroom. Then he'd crawl, like a wounded animal, back to his hole.

---

[8] These are Lester's words, as he told the story to his follower and associate Virginia Lloyd. Virginia wrote a wonderful book on Lester's life that is titled *Choose Freedom,* with many quotes by Lester in it. It was published by Freedom Publications of Phoenix, Arizona in 1983. The book is now out of print, but it is so well done, I have decided to reprint it in the near future.

On the fourth day, something changed. After his midday meal he was sitting in a chair, looking out the window at Central Park. There was snow; the trees were sparkling; the park looked like a fairyland. He was thinking of how beautiful it was and then realized that he wasn't enjoying it at all. He could not respond, even to beauty. He was a virtual invalid with no hope of ever getting any better. At best, he could look forward to years of sitting in this apartment, nursing a frail corpse that hadn't the good sense to lie down and get it over with. That thought made him so furious he got up from his chair with the greatest surge of energy he'd had since his attack, went straight to the medicine chest in the bathroom and counted his pills. He found a good supply of the newer medications; sedatives and heart pills.

There were also morphine tablets a doctor had prescribed some years before for the pain of kidney stones. There were certainly enough left in the bottle to take him off this planet if you just floated off on a warm, cozy cloud, everything rosy. It was certainly better than waiting for another heart attack.

Okay. Now he had a choice. For the first time since his illness, he felt he had some control over what happened to him. He considered what to do. Should he take the pills now and get it over with? No, not right now, he decided; he could always take them when and if things got too bad.

He went back to his chair and began looking the situation over, speaking aloud to himself, "You're still breathing. No matter what those doctors or anyone else says about the prognosis, you're still breathing, and that's what counts. Maybe there's some hope after all."

"Okay, where do I start?" That question brought on the sinking feeling again, and it occurred to him that perhaps he should go ahead and take the pills at once. At least then he'd be out of his misery and could stop fighting. And what had he been fighting for all his life anyway? Just a little happiness, that was all; and he hadn't found it, not ever, not in any way that lasted more than a few minutes or hours at a time. Momentary. That's what life was. Momentary... impermanent; always changing; you'd no sooner think you had it made, had everything nailed down and could relax, than the next thing would happen and there you were, right back where you'd started, clutching, clutching, clutching for something you couldn't hold even if you got it. What the hell was life all about anyway?

What was it all about? What *was* he doing here on this planet? It didn't make any sense to him that he should be born; go through all he had gone through in his life; never really get anywhere that really mattered; and end up with nothing, absolutely nothing except a dying body and eventually even that turns to dust. All his possessions and accomplishments felt meaningless and empty. "Like dust," he thought.

"Ashes to ashes and dust to dust...
If the war doesn't get you, the taxes must."

He had to laugh at the truth in that silly rhyme. Life seemed so stupid. But as he thought about taking the pills, he realized that he couldn't give up yet. There was something stirring in the back of his mind, an elusive thought that there might be an answer if only he knew where to look. Well, he had nothing but time, he figured, and even though his body was half dead, he still had his mind; he could still think.

"Should I try?" he wondered aloud.

For a moment, he wavered then, decided with a shrug, "Oh, what the hell, I got nothing to lose. If it doesn't work, I can always take the pills." And he knew he would if it came to that. There was no doubt in his mind.

That being settled, he didn't have to think about it again. His mind felt clearer than it had in a long time, and for the first time since his illness, he felt truly hungry. He went to the kitchen and fixed himself a real meal. Still very weak, he took his time and didn't try to rush. As he ate, his mind was busy exploring new thoughts, questions, ideas of where to look for his answer. The new project was exciting and he felt himself coming alive again.

Refreshed and strengthened by the meal, he went back to his chair by the window "Where to begin?" he wondered, "Well, first, what are the questions?"

"What is life? What is it about? Is there a reason for my being here in this world, and if so, what is it?" He looked in the dictionary, he tried Freud, but no, Freud had no answers for him. He went on to others; Watson's Behaviorism, Jung and Adler, nothing for him in those, either.

Then there were the philosophers. He began taking books from the shelves, putting them in a pile. He'd read them all cover to cover more than once; maybe he'd missed something. After all, he thought, he hadn't then had specific questions. Taking books to his chair by the window, he began to read. He skimmed through one after the other, stopping to read paragraphs or pages here and there.

His head began to feel clogged with information, and his thoughts were spinning. Becoming increasingly impatient, he went back to the shelves for other books, books on medicine, physics and engineering. He had books on everything and he looked through them all over the next two days. The room was a mess, books piled everywhere, some lying open on the floor where he had thrown them in his frustration. The only ones left on the shelves were a joke book and some biographies, which had been given to him as gifts.

Where to look next? "You were always a smart boy," he told himself. "Didn't you win a full scholarship to

Rutgers by competitive exams when there were only three being given? Even though you were a Jew, they couldn't hold that back from you. You won it!

And in school, weren't you always on the honor roll? And had read tons of stuff on man, from engineering and physics to psychiatry and philosophy and medicine?

"Well, if you're so smart, big shot, what did all that study and knowledge and readings get you? Migraines, kidney stones, ulcers, appendicitis, pain, misery, unhappiness, and finally a coronary which should have finished you off and didn't. What more do you need before you come to your senses?

"For a smart boy, Lester, you are stupid, stupid, stupid! All that knowledge has availed you nothing. And here you are looking for more, wanting more books written by someone else who hasn't found the answers either."

"That's that!" he told himself. "I'm finished with all that crap."

With that decision, he felt a lifetime burden lift from his shoulders. Suddenly, he felt light, almost giddy. He realized he had actually been looking for the same answers all his life, but now he knew, without a doubt, that if they were to be found in any of the conventional places, he would have already found them. He would have to look somewhere else. And he thought he knew where.

He would put all that useless knowledge aside, disregard everything he'd learned, go back to the lab and start from scratch. The problems were within him, he reasoned. It was his body, his mind, his emotions. The answers must be within him, too. That was his lab and that's where he would look. It felt good. He went to his chair and began his search.

For a month he sat, relentlessly questioning, probing. At first, he tried to obey doctor's orders and spend a good part of each day resting in bed but he couldn't stick with it. His mind was too active, and this new research was the most exciting thing he had ever done. He worked at it as intensely as he had worked on other projects, by trial and experience. He had two-way conversations with himself, first posing a question, then exploring each possible answer until he could either validate it or eliminate it. By doing this, he made his first big breakthrough; got the first real answer.

It was about a month after he'd begun his self-search, and he was looking into the question of happiness. He'd already eliminated some answers and once again asked himself, "What is happiness?"

The answer that came was this, "Happiness is when you're being loved." That seemed simple enough.

He went on. "Okay, would you say you are happy now? Do you feel happy?"

The answer was no.

"Okay," was the conclusion... "then that must mean you are not loved!"

"Well, that's not exactly true," came the rebuttal. "Your family loves you."

That made him stop and think. He saw again their concerned faces when he'd been so sick in the hospital, remembered the pleasure in their eyes when he'd returned home after each lengthy sojourn elsewhere, heard his sister Doris' sweet voice on the telephone, "How are you, honey?" Oh, yes, he was loved. There was no mistake about that.

And there were women, too. He could think of more than one who would marry him in a minute if he asked. He knew it was so because they had asked him, and had broken off the relationship when he refused.

There were men who loved him, too, as a friend. These were men he had known all his life, real friends who had stood by him through all kinds of difficulties, who still called regularly just to say hello and see how he was doing, who enjoyed spending time with him. They loved him.

It came as a shock that with all that love, he still wasn't happy. It became obvious that being loved was not the answer to happiness. He threw it out and tried a new approach.

"Maybe happiness lies in accomplishments," he thought. He remembered when he'd won the Rutgers scholarship, when Kelvinator had upped his salary, when he got his first apartment, when he opened the first Hitching Post, when he made the coup in Canadian lumber. Proud of himself, yes, But happy? No, not what he would call happy.

"Well then," he asked himself, "have I ever been happy, and if so, when?"

The first part was easy; of course, he'd been happy sometimes, but when, specifically? He began to look at it... there were the summer times years ago when he was camping out with the fellows. He had been happy then. Oh, not every minute, of course, so what were the specific moments? The first thing that flashed into his mind was a picture of him helping his friend, Sy, put up his tent one summer. Sy had arrived late in the afternoon and one of his tent ropes had broken. Lester had helped him, both of them laughing, pleased with their friendship, feeling good about themselves and each other. He had been happy then. He chuckled at the memory. He felt good even now, thinking about it.

"What were some other times?" he asked, and the next thing he remembered was how he felt when his friend, Milton, had eloped in college. No one was supposed to know about it, but Milton had told his best friend, Lester. He had been very happy then; was it because he felt special that Milton had told him a secret? Upon reflection he saw that it wasn't that. No, it was the expression on Milton's face, talking about his beautiful new bride and how much he loved her; they just didn't want to wait until after college. Lester had felt a twinge of envy for a moment, but then had looked closely at his friend's face beaming with love and he knew he had definitely been happy for Milton. He felt the happiness well up in him even now, after all the years, as he sat with eyes closed, reviewing the scene in his mind. Yes, he had been happy then.

As he continued to review the past, happy times came faster and faster. He remembered June and driving to pick her up for a date, his heart singing with love, impatient to see her. He had been happy then.

And there was Nettie. Oh, God, he hadn't thought about her for such a long time. He really didn't want to now, there was so much pain attached to it, but there it was. He'd been running away from that pain all his life it seemed, and he was tired, tired of running. It was the end of the line and he simply couldn't run any longer. So he forced himself to look and to question.

Oh, yes, he had been happy with Nettie. Memories flashed through his mind, moments when he had held her in his arms so tenderly, wanting to take her right inside himself. Moments at parties, when he would unexpectedly catch her eye across a room and be flooded with love. Remembering her smile, the sun glinting on her hair, the serious look on her face as they sat studying together, the faint flowery smell of her, the sound of her laughter, her voice soft in the night, "I love you, Lester."

He sat back and let the pictures flood him, wash over him, let it all flow, let the long-held pain flow. His heart ached until his carefully erected, protected dam broke and for the first time, he cried over his lost love, his Nettie, his darling. Grief seemed to come from some bottomless pit of pain and loneliness. It went on for what seemed like hours and when it was over, he felt drained and weak. When he could, he crept from the chair to his bed and slept like a dead man.

***

In the morning, he woke very early feeling rested and refreshed. His first thought was, "Well, then, what is happiness?" He laughed at his tenacity as he rolled out of bed and into the shower. Preparing breakfast, his thoughts continued to explore the question which dominated his mind.

Well, then, what is happiness? What is the common denominator in all these moments? There was Sy, there was Milton, then June, and his Nettie... What was the common denominator? Somehow he knew it was tied up with love, but he could not, at first, see how. When it finally came, it was so simple and pure and complete an answer that he wondered why he had never seen it before.

"Happiness is when I am loving!" He realized that in every instance, his feeling of love for the other person had been intense and that's where the happiness had come from, from his own feeling of loving.

It was so clear to him now that being loved was not the answer. He could see that even if people loved him, unless he felt love in return, he was not going to be happy. Their loving might make them happy, but it would not, could not, make him happy. It was a new and mind-boggling concept and even though he instinctively knew that it was correct, his old scientific training didn't allow him to accept it without testing. So he looked into his past, remembering those times in his life when he had been loving and happy, and he recognized that at those times, the other person had not necessarily been loving him.

He looked at the other side too, the unhappy times and now that he knew what to look for, it was very obvious that he had not been loving. Oh, he'd thought at the time that he loved them, as with Nettie and June. He loved them, needed them, wanted them. But was that love, he wondered now? No, it was painful... he was experiencing pain that they didn't love him. And even though he called it love, he was really wanting to possess them completely, thinking he needed all their love to be happy.

That was the key! He had been experiencing a want or lack of love, expecting the other person to supply the love, waiting for the other person to *make* him happy. He had to laugh, it seemed so ludicrous. To think that someone else could make him happy seemed like the funniest thing in the world. He knew, better than anyone that no one could ever make him anything. He'd always been very proud and stubborn and self-sufficient, sure that he never needed anyone or anything. "What a joke!" He thought. The truth is that he'd been all the time dying inside for want of love, thinking he had to get it from someone. Tears rolled down his cheeks as he laughed and laughed at the realization that what he'd been looking for all his life was inside him. He had been like the absent-minded professor looking everywhere for his glasses which were on top of his head all the time.

"What a shame," he thought, wiping away the tears. "What a shame that I never saw this before. All that time, all those years wasted; what a shame."

"But wait a minute!" he thought. "If happiness is when I'm experiencing love for the other one, then that means happiness is a feeling within me.

"And if I felt unloving in the past? Well, I know I can't change the past, but could I possibly correct the feeling now inside myself? Could I change the feeling to love now?" He decided to try it. He looked at his most recent unhappiness, the day he left the hospital.

"First," he asked himself, "was I experiencing a lack of love that day?"

"Yes," he answered aloud. "Nobody gave a damn about me, not the nurses, not the orderlies, not even Dr. Schultz. They did not care. As sick as I was, they threw me out, sent me home to die so they wouldn't have to watch one of their failures. Well, the hell with them. They can all go to hell." He was shocked at the vehemence in his voice. His body trembled with rage and he felt weak. He really hated the doctor. He could feel it burning in his chest. "Oh, boy," he thought," this sure isn't love."

"Well, can I change it?" he asked. "Is it possible to turn it into love for the doctor?"

"Hell, no," he thought, "why should I? What did he ever do to deserve any love?"

"That's not the point," he answered himself. "The point is not whether he deserves love. The point is, can you do it? Is it possible to simply change a feeling of hatred into a feeling of love—not for the benefit of the other person but for yourself?"

As the thought crossed his mind, he felt something break loose in his chest. A gentle easing, a sense of dissolving, and the burning sensation was gone. He didn't trust it at first. It seemed too easy, so he pictured again the scene with Dr. Schultz in the hospital. He was surprised to find that it brought only a mild feeling of resentment rather than the previous intense burning hatred. He wondered if he could do it again.

"Let's see," he thought, "what did I just do? Ah, yes. Can I change this feeling of resentment into a feeling of love?" He chuckled as he felt the resentment dissolve in his chest. Then it was totally gone and he was happy. He thought of Dr. Schultz again, pictured him in his mind and felt happy, even loving. He saw now, reliving that last meeting, how the doctor had hated to tell him the things he had to say. He could feel the doctor's pain at having to tell a young man in the prime of his life that his life was over. "Doctor Schultz, you son-of-a-gun," he said, grinning, "I love you."

"Well, it worked on that one," he thought. "If my theory is sound, then it should work on everything." Eagerly, he began trying it on other moments, and the results were consistently the same, each time that he asked himself if he could change the feeling of hostility or anger or hatred to one of love, the dissolving process took place. Sometimes he had to repeat it over and over until he felt only Love for the person. At times, the entire process would take only a minute or two; at other times, it might take him hours of working on a particular person or event before his feelings were only loving, but he would doggedly stay with it until it was completed on each person and each incident.

His entire life came up for review in bits and pieces. One by one, he changed to Love all the old hurts and disappointments. He began to feel stronger as the weight of his pain dropped away. He was happier than he had ever been in his entire life, and he kept it going, feeling even more happiness with each new thing corrected.

He stopped going to bed because he had so much energy that he couldn't lie down. When he felt tired, he would doze in his chair and awaken an hour or so later to start in again. There was so much to be corrected in his life that he didn't want to stop until he had looked under every stone and around every corner.

Another thing that intrigued him was the question of how far he could take this. As he corrected each thing, he became happier, he could feel it; but he wondered how far he could go. Was there a limit to happiness? So far, he hadn't found any boundaries to it and the possibilities were staggering. So he kept on, around the clock.

His strength was returning, but not wanting to be distracted, he avoided getting involved in social activities and would sometimes even pass up the Sunday get-together with his family. He did his food shopping in the middle of the night, around two or three in the morning. There were very few people up and about at that hour, and he enjoyed the quiet of the city. He went on correcting his life, even while doing the necessaries. And he noticed that when someone in a store or on the street would annoy him, he was able to correct that response with Love either immediately or shortly thereafter. This pleased him, and he found himself loving others with intensity far beyond anything he had imagined possible. As he described it many years later, "When I mixed with people, and again and again when they would do things that I didn't like and within me was a feeling of non-Love, I would immediately change that attitude to one of loving them even though they were opposing me. Eventually I got to a point where, no matter how much I was being opposed, I could maintain a feeling of Love for them.

He continued to correct his life with consistent results for about a month until one day he got stumped. He was working on the last time he had seen Nettie, the day she chose someone else. He had already corrected a lot of the pain with regard to her; she had come to his mind again and again, and it had not always been easy. In fact, it had been very difficult at first to work on that old relationship but gradually as he gained strength, he had been able to confront some of those long-buried feelings and correct them.

But on this particular day, no matter how hard he tried to correct it with Love, there was still a feeling of despair which he could not dislodge. He wanted to escape, to get out of his chair and run, to get something to eat, to do anything that would get him away from his intense feeling. Instead, he decided to sit there until he handled it. Something told him that if he let that feeling push him around, if he lost that battle, he would have lost the war. He stayed in his chair, determined to ride it out.

He probed, "What's wrong here? Why isn't it dissolving? Nettie, oh, my Nettie." He began to cry now, tears streaming down his cheeks, all the pain he had locked up on the day they parted came now in a flood. "Why did you do it, Nettie?" he cried aloud. "Why did you do it? Why did you leave me, my darling? We could have been so happy, we'd have married and been so happy."

"Damn," he thought, "why do people do things like that? They throw their happiness away and everyone else's, too. They have no right to do that. They shouldn't be allowed to do that. There should be some way of making them change; some way of changing the things they do and the effect they have on people."

He felt the old pain of ulcers starting up again in his stomach and realized with certainty that the ulcers had started that last day with Nettie. He'd drunk the beer and thrown up; that had been the beginning. He wished it had been different. More than anything else in this world, he wanted to change what had happened. He wanted to go back and live it over again the other way with Nettie choosing him, with them getting married and being happy forevermore.

"Well, you can't change it, stupid," he shouted at himself, "so you might just as well stop trying to." That jolted him. He saw that he was still trying to change something that had been finished more than twenty years ago.

"No, it can't be finished," he cried. "I won't let it be finished." His throat hurt now and he felt like screaming and smashing things.

Then, like instant replay, he heard what he'd said, "I won't let it be finished." That was the source of his anguish; he'd wanted to change it all these years and so he kept it alive inside himself, buried deep, eroding his happiness.

"Well, to hell with that," he said, almost flippantly. Suddenly, with that decision, the whole thing was gone. He couldn't believe it. He felt for the hurt, the pain, the despair. It was all gone. He thought of Nettie as he remembered her, so young, so beautiful, and he simply loved her. There was none of the old painful feeling left.

***

He began to look now in this new direction. He realized that the cause of his ulcers was that he had wanted to change everything, starting with his nearest and dearest and extending out to the rest of the world, including the United States, other countries, government heads, the weather, endings of movies he had seen, the way businesses were run, taxes, the army, the President; there was nothing he could think of that he had not wanted to change in one way or another.

What a revelation! He saw himself subject to and a victim of everything he wanted to change! He began dissolving all that. When he thought of something that caused him pain about a person or situation, he would now either correct it with Love or dissolve wanting to change it.

This added a new dimension to his work, and his progress accelerated. By the time a second month had gone by, it was all he could do sometimes to stay in his chair, he became so energized. And there were times, when he had worked on particularly painful incidents in his life, that he literally could not sit and would go out into the city and walk for miles, reviewing, correcting, dissolving until he had burned off enough energy to sit still again.

Sometimes he felt as though he had hold of a chain with many links of incidents on it which needed correcting. Once he got hold of the chain, he would follow through incident by incident until there was nothing left to be corrected. An example of such a chain was jealousy.

He had always been intensely jealous but managed to hide it most of the time under a facade of not caring. Nevertheless, his insides used to burn if the girl he was with so much as looked at someone else, or even mentioned another man. He decided to correct this tendency in himself. He would probe his memory for instances where his jealousy had driven him; correct it; then look for more. When he thought it was cleared out, he tested himself by imagining the girl he loved most making love with the man he would least want her to be with. It was a good test because he could see immediately that there was more work to do. Sometimes the intensity of his feelings would almost drive him mad, but he continued for days until there was no last vestige of jealousy left in him. When he could finally enjoy their enjoyment of each other, he knew he was finished with jealousy.

Insights came with increasing frequency He would often gain a sudden, complete understanding of something which had always puzzled him. Philosophies he had studied became clear, and he could see that they had often started off on the right track, only to veer off into distortions, having been diverted by an incorrect idea springing from the author's own storehouse of uncorrected feelings.

His mind began to feel like crystal, clear and sharp. Colors seemed brighter and everything was more sharply defined, says Lester.

"Above all, I saw that I was responsible for everything that had happened to me, formerly thinking that the world was abusing me! And I saw that my tremendous effort to make money and then losing it was due only to my thinking; that I had been always seeking happiness, and thought that making money would do it. So whenever the business started to make money, and the money did not bring me the happiness I wanted, I began to lose interest and the thing collapsed. I had always blamed it on other people and circumstances, not realizing that it was simply my subconscious knowledge that this is not happiness which caused me to lose interest and that, in turn, caused the business to collapse.

"This was a tremendous piece of freedom, to think that I am not a victim of this world, that it lies within my power to arrange the world the way I want it to be; that rather than be an effect of it, I can now be in control of it and arrange it the way I would like it to be. That was a tremendous realization, a tremendous feeling of Freedom.

"Discovering that my happiness equated to my loving, and that my thinking was the cause of things happening to me in my life gave me more and more freedom; freedom from the subconscious compulsions that I had to work, I had to make money, I had to have girlfriends. Freedom in the feeling that I was now able to determine my destiny, I was now able to control my world, lightened my internal burden so strongly that I felt there was no need for me to have to do anything.

"Plus, this happiness was so great. It was a new experience for me. I was experiencing a joy that I never knew existed, never dreamed could be. So I decided, "This is so great, I'm not going to stop until I carry it all the way." I had no idea how far it could go. I had no idea how joyous a person could be. But I was determined to find out. "

During the third month, things went even faster. There was a depth to Lester's feelings that threatened to bowl him over at times. His knees sometimes buckled, but he stayed with each feeling until it was corrected.

He was becoming happier and happier, still looking to see if there were any limits to what he could accomplish with this new process. "How much further can I go?" Lester would ask himself, then push it even further.

It was also during the third month that he ran into an old adversary, one he had seen out of the corner of his eye again and again throughout his life. It had lurked nearby, always on the periphery and he had never before been willing to meet it head on. It was the fear of death.

Now he recognized it as the basis of every single feeling he had ever had. He began to coax it out into the open, wanting to take a good look at this biggest foe of all, which had so very nearly won the battle only a few months ago. He began to lure those feelings into the open and to dissolve them. And it worked!

He got to the place where, with great confidence, he laughed and laughed and laughed at this foe which had kept a fire lit under him his entire life so that there had not been one moment of real peace, ever. This last of the monsters turned out to be, after all, only a feeling.

As he dissolved the fear of death, he realized one day that his body was sound, healed. The physical impairment was corrected. He couldn't explain to anyone how he knew; he just knew it as surely as he knew who he was. His body was sound.

In the end of the third month, he had slipped into a blissful, joyous state, which he could only describe as feeling like a million orgasms surging all at once through his entire body. It went on and on and he realized that this feeling, although not sexual, was what he was always been looking for but never found in sex. He felt light, living for weeks with joy exploding inside him every moment. Everyone and everything became exquisitely beautiful to him. He kept looking for more things to correct, but there didn't seem to be much. Occasionally something would occur to him, but it would be gone almost before he could define it and the joy would surge through him even more strongly

After several weeks, he began to wonder if there could be anything better beyond this joy. He was sitting in his chair in the usual position, slumped down, legs stretched out, chin touching his chest. He had an idle thought without expecting an answer, but the answer came.

What was beyond this incredible joyous state that didn't stop? He saw that it was peace, imperturbability and he realized with certainty that if he accepted it, if he decided to move into that peace, it would never, ever go away. And he went—slipped into it so effortlessly—with just a <u>decision</u>[9] to have it. He was there.

Everything was still. He was in a quietness that he now knew had always been there but drowned out by incessant noise from his accumulated, uncorrected past. In fact, it was more than quiet; it was so far beyond

---

[9] Underlining is mine, in order once again to emphasize incredible power of Irrevocable Decision.

anything imaginable that there were no words to describe the delectable deliciousness of the tranquility.

His earlier question about happiness was answered too. There were no limits to happiness, but when you have it all, every minute, it gets tiresome. Then this peace is just beyond and all you have to do is step over the line into it.

"Is there anything beyond even this?" he wondered. But as he asked, he knew the answer.

This peace was eternal and forever and it was the essence of every living thing. There was only one *Beingness* and everything was *It*. Every person was *It*, but they were without awareness of the fact, blinded by the uncorrected past they hold on to.

Awareness, Oneness

Up from Earth's center through the seventh gate
I rose, and on the throne of Saturn sate,
And many knots unraveled by the road;
But not the knot of human death and fate.

We are the body and mind, but our essence is *Awareness*. To realize this, we need to let go of limitations that we created with concepts and feelings.

Beyond time and space exists an immeasurable ocean of *Awareness* — the Source — an unknown intelligence. In unfathomable depths of Awareness appear all forms of life: a glorious incomprehensible illusion called Universe. Not only does our Universe reside in this miraculous ocean of Awareness; there are countless numbers of other universes forming infinite universal systems. The boundless ocean of

Awareness contains and provides life to all existence. From all times voices come to us from different cultures, says Leo Hartong in his book *Awakening to the Dream*, from east and west, north and south, some many centuries apart, yet all pointing in the same direction and sometimes literarily saying the same thing.

Here are a few concrete examples:

Christianity: *For behold the Kingdom of God is within you.*
Luke 17:21
Buddhism: *You are all buddhas. There is nothing you need to achieve.*
Just open your eyes (Sidhartha Gautama)
Zen: *If you cannot find the truth right where you are, where else you expect to find it?* (Dogen Zenji)
Taoism: Great *knowledge sees all in one. Small knowledge breaks down into the many.* (Chuang Tzu)
Science: *Bell's theorem demonstrates that the universe is fundamentally interconnected, interdependent and inseparable.* (Fritjof Capra)
Tibetan Buddhism: *There is not a single state that is not this vast state of presence.*
Islam: *'In that glory is no 'I' or 'We' or 'Thou.' 'I', 'We', 'Thou' and 'He' are all one thing'* (Hallaj)
Hinduism: *Tat Tvan Asi – Thou Art That.*
Judaism: *I am That I am.*

All these expressions point to the fact that all is one, that this is IT, and that you are IT. Why then in this book we call 'IT' Awareness? Become silent and look within. The world is gone, but what is left? Withdraw your attention from your body, from outside and inside… what is left? Awareness that is aware of itself. No matter how much you withdrew your attention from everything within and without, you are always aware. As a matter of fact the more you withdraw, the more you become aware. No words, no thoughts, all limitations that created illusion called mind are gone, everything is gone, except Awareness.

Intelligence has been defined in many different ways, including the abilities for abstract thought, understanding, communication, reasoning, learning, planning, emotional intelligence and problem solving. However, in this book, Intelligence means the ability to be aware. I came to this realization based on people's general belief in the Unknown Intelligence, whether it is called Universal Mind, God, The Unknown, Emptiness, Awareness, the Source or any other name. Thus, the highly intelligent person is capable of being highly aware, and, of course, is capable of better understanding, better communicating, learning, planning, solving problems and much more.

Awareness is forever and the more you are aware, more oneness you experience with all that is. This is best experienced in deep meditation. Though state of Awareness is a very personal experience and cannot be conveyed with words, described indirectly, Awareness is intuitive perception ourselves being true Love and Oneness with all universe. Of course, our subconscious and our genes affect our ability to be aware, but *when we destroy walls*, says Tao, *we will live in a garden*. Our essence is incomparably more powerful than limitations that we superimposed on Awareness or information carried by genes, and our Irrevocable Decision[10] to break down the walls of ignorance or limitations cannot be cancelled by anything.

Our essence Awareness is always the same changeless ocean that is aware of itself in all that is. Being beyond all

---

[10] For more information on nature of the Irrevocable Decision see chapter *Decision and Mind Control.*

known dimensions, it contains all dimensions, all universes and beyond. Awareness is our essence and we can realize our essence as true Love, because in its highest expression love becomes true Love, which is the closest possible state to Awareness that we could experience while in the body. The less we are limited, the closer we are to 'IT'—our essence or Self, to our center, our home. How do we achieve this realization? We start moving closer to our Self, when we begin to let go of the limitations that we superimposed over our true Love).

Bodhidharma, who traveled to China in the sixth century, was first Zen patriarch in that country. Even today in China, Nepal and India Bodhidharma is considered on par with Buddha. Says Bodhidharma:

"If you see your nature, you don't need to read sutras. Erudition and knowledge are not only useless, but also cloud your awareness. Doctrines are only for pointing to your nature. Once you see your nature, why pay attention to doctrines?

"To go from a mortal to a Buddha, you have to nurture awareness, and accept what life brings. If you're often getting angry, you'll turn yourself against the way. Once people see their nature, all attachments end. Awareness isn't hidden, but you can only find it right now. It's only now. Once you nurture Awareness, any attachments that remain will come to an end. Understanding comes naturally. You don't have to make any effort."

When emperor Vu asked Bodhidharma what is the first principle of the holy teachings, Bodhidharma replied: *Emptiness, none holiness.* The emperor did not understand but asked another question: "Who stands before me?" *No-knowledge.* Said Bodhidharma. Emperor didn't comprehend the meaning of these words either. But in these words concentrates entire meaning of Zen and the

Way, which says there is no Way, as there are no ways to the Self. We are already home; no way is necessary to get there. *Emptiness, no holiness* means there is no need for teachings, doctrines, scriptures... it is all created by someone. There is you and nature: trees, grass, mountains and oceans. It is enough to be in silence among trees dancing in the wind. You don't need other information, you don't need any information. Just dance in wordless knowledge together with trees. This is your experience, your life, but as soon as you would try to put it in words, it is dead, because it can only be lived.

This is why I live amidst nature and take everyday walk in the mountains. I hug pines and bow before oaks, and if by accident I step on a little wild flower, I wish to kill myself, because flowers are eyes—the eyes of nature —my own eyes.

When we come home we know that there was no way. We know we have always been home, that we are home – boundless ocean of Awareness or Mind, which is not obstructed by dogmas and doctrines, concepts and emotions and is shared by all people. This is why in this book 'IT' is called Awareness (Mind, with a capital 'M').

The idea of the movie screen may be used in order to illustrate Awareness. Whatever is happening on the screen does not harm or affect it. When just another show is finished, the screen is the same. The difference between movie screen and Awareness is that movie screen is two-dimensional while Awareness is beyond the concept of dimension. However, whatever is happening within the boundless 'ocean' of Awareness, cannot affect it. Wars, shells and A-bombs cannot damage it, cold cannot shrink it, fire cannot burn it. How do we know this? Because, no matter what's going on in the world, including human and natural cataclysms, at all times, there always live those who are free, the wise, who are highly aware. If

Awareness could be damaged in any way, there, by now, would be no people who are supremely aware, there would be no world either, as there would be no provider of life.

What is Oneness? Is it an oneness with God, with people, with nature? May be it is a Oneness with the Universe, with all that is? If it is with all that is, does it mean that I am also one with some murderer or people like Hitler, Lenin and alike? Many people do not feel, to be one with others, but it doesn't destroy Oneness. When the veil of ignorance is lifted with releasing the blocks, we realize we are one with everyone else, with all that is. Oneness is readiness to become aware and to accept every detail in the universe, every person, all concepts and ideas of humanity.

On our inner level we are one, despite difference in attitudes and opinions. Despite our feelings of love and hate, aversions and attachments, likes and dislikes, we are one. When we are in love... even if our intelligence is low, we are still experiencing oneness, though not always realizing it. It happens, because every kind of love is rooted in true Love, which is oneness.

Take a look at your life. The events there, are changing like in kaleidoscope. Recently you were child, yesterday—youth, and today you are already a parent or grandparent and soon, very soon you will be no one, your acting role will end. Meanwhile, a whirlpool of endless changes is happening to you and around you. Everything is continually changing, including your body and mind. But do we really change? The inner quiet, does it ever change?

It is not unusual to hear from a person of any age: "I feel like twenty!" Our minds are always old and are getting older, so are our bodies, but something within every one of us is always young, ageless, changeless.

What is it? It is an inner quiet—a changeless state of peace, of quietude that we all have, but not just us. Though not aware, every animal has it, every blade of grass, every tree and flower has it: Awareness that is aware of itself in all that exists and provides life to all that lives... is this quiet, this peace.

Thoughts are assaulting us without mercy. Now they are thoughts of happiness, now they are sad thoughts of illness, problems, dilemmas. But in between the thoughts there are always seemingly imperceptible moments of quietude. These moments are always the same, soothing, relaxing—forever the same. Feelings, thoughts, emotions differ from person to person, but not these moments of quiet: they are all the same to everyone. This is our immortal changeless Awareness, a state of peace, which knows no change. It is because of this Awareness, this state of changeless center that we are able to perceive change.

We shed, our bodies the same way we change our clothes, cars and homes, but our quietude of peace, our essence Awareness is immortal and is the same in everyone: it is shared by all that is.

Everyone knows he is aware. It is at this level that everything, everyone is one, is Awareness or pure Mind that is always present right behind our concepts, ideas, thoughts, emotions... behind conditioning.

The Nature of Want, Resistance, Fear and Releasing

Come, fill the cup, and in the fire of Spring
The winter garment of repentance fling;
The bird of time has but a little way
To fly—and lo! The bird is on the wing.

Awareness is our natural state. In order to be closer to the center or more aware, it is necessary to empty oneself of the accumulated garbage. When truly released, we are peaceful loving and happy. Peace, Love is the absence of apathy, grief, fear jealousy, anger and other negativity. Peace is loving. The less limited we are by negative thoughts and feelings, the more aware, loving and happier we are.

Releasing of the accumulated negativity can be as effective as meditation. Releasing does away with limitations and naturally leads to a state of peace. I saw releasing being nucleus of every important teaching of the past, where it was called 'purification' or 'cleansing'.

Goal of releasing is a life of happiness; its intermediate aim is learning how to bear and transcend misery, solve problems and achieve goals.

It is true that we already are free beings, and need only to become aware of it. This "only" makes all the difference, however, because to become aware of being free, most of us need to learn releasing and/or meditation. Jesus went to India and Tibet where he meditated and studied under various teachers. Buddha was meditating for six years and studied under different teachers before he realized Freedom, so were Bodhidharma, Lahiri Mahasaya,

Huang Po, Swami Sri Yukteswar, Paramahanza Yogananda and other men of wisdom.

This is how it happened to Buddha. He was sitting under a tree, doing nothing, completely relaxed. Six years of superhuman effort had passed and brought him only disappointment. He did everything possible: fasting, yoga, breathing exercises... he tried every technique known in India. He did it all. He almost died while fasting. That evening he was so tired and so disappointed. "All is in vain," he thought, "world is empty—I saw this emptiness." His father was a king. "I renounced the world—there is no meaning in it. And now I am giving up all this useless asceticism. I'm giving up all search, for this too, is nonsense. There is nothing that is worth finding, nothing at all. Every effort is but vanity."

Only utter disappointment may kill one's efforts in search of truth.

Suddenly, it happened.

Early morning he opened his eyes and saw the last star vanishing in the sky; and like that star, something within him—last remains of self-image—also vanished. The doer was no more. And at that very moment an entire creation downed upon him.

The teachings and meditation effort was to Buddha a six year long stepping stone—transition into effortlessness. Freedom is free from effort. Awareness is effortless, harmony is effortless, Love is effortless. With effort you may hate, you may accomplish goals, because effort means aggression, it means violence, force, constraint, competition. Illusion of resistance creates effort. Nothing can be gained through effort in the spiritual world, and those who began with effort, eventually discarded it. However, if you can throw out effort in the beginning, you would no longer need the techniques, because every technique employs effort to undo effort, to 'move' you beyond effort.

When spring arrives, grass appears by itself, says Zen. This is the way of effortlessness, not of the effort, not of fighting and striving. But to come to that point, Buddha had spent six years of great effort, fighting and striving.

Nevertheless, there are always exceptions. Lester Levenson knew nothing about teachings and meditation. He went free in three short months of the very intense releasing. Of course, these three months were a time of great effort of releasing all negativity, accumulated during 43 years of his life and converting each negative feeling and thought into Love.

Freedom knows no method, no techniques. You've made no effort to be born, nor does your breathing require any effort. Everything needs to be let to happen naturally, as if all by itself, as your birth and your breathing. Understand this and you don't need to practice, because with this understanding you've made the transition into a life of higher awareness. But this would require allowing life to flow, and for you to effortlessly flow with it, letting the stream of life to carry you wherever it goes. Your complete trust in life would require no plans, no destination.

This means to be natural, to be in harmony with nature, with all life, to accept whatever life brings and to trust that unobstructed, life would bring you all you need to grow in awareness, it would give you everything you need when you need it. You need to add nothing to it and nothing to subtract, for nature and life are perfect and need no improvement.

The amount of time and effort leading to effortlessness of Freedom, cannot be determined in advance. Like nature, Freedom is beyond planning. All you could do is to courageously plunge head on into the ocean of the unknown, and swim away from the shore until all effort is spent.

Whom the gods would destroy they first make mad, says an old adage. But people do not care that they harbor negative thoughts and emotions, because among other reasons, they believe it is human. Yet, life is free of negativity. Negativity is humanity's sickness; it is nothing but a point of view—an illusion rooted in the fear of death. *See no evil, hear no evil, do no evil and there will be no evil.* You certainly could avoid doing evil, but it is difficult to avoid seeing and hearing evil. However, no matter what you see and hear, no matter how bad it is, you must be calm inwardly. *See no evil, hear no evil* is witnessing all that goes before you with no negativity arising within you. Witnessing is impartial. We know it when we are highly aware. When we are highly aware, we become a true witness, because when we are highly aware, we are in the center, we are home, where there is no negativity and we *see no evil, hear no evil* when free, so it cannot affect our state of tranquility. In our nature of Pure Awareness we are only witnessing all that goes around, we are not participating. True witnessing is a state of *Pure Awareness*, a state of Freedom.

It is not *evil* that enslaves and makes our life miserable, but the associated negativity, which we unknowingly accept when we *see evil* and *hear evil* being in a state of ignorance.

When something makes us feel angry, it means that anger already was stored within; an outside event was only a trigger. Our reaction to the world is a good indicator of what we are harboring within. When free, nothing in the outside world can disturb us. We can experience feelings, but so imperturbable is our inner peace, no feeling can ever affect it.

The purpose of the thinking process is to create; thusly the negative thinking pattern will eventually result in negative circumstances. Low awareness prevents people from recognizing this simple fact: whatever they willingly or unsuspectingly "download" to their subconscious mind via thought and feeling has a good chance of becoming their experience.

Not aware of the mind's tremendous creative power, people mistreat their thinking process, even when using it as a communication tool. Because they are unable to handle this wonderful servant, it runs loose and creates chaos. When we learn how to keep in mind only what we wish to experience in life, and release all else, we begin to steer our life in a desired direction.

***

WANT is a paradox. To obtain something, it is important to WANT it. However WANT means lack of what you want. The more you WANT something, the more you affirm the lack of it. It is better not to WANT but to allow whatever you need to come to you. Otherwise WANT will sabotage you, becoming a block, a barrier. At the start, WANT is an accelerator, soon after that, it becomes a brake. But you don't know when this happens, and will be driving your goal-car with both the accelerator and brakes on. And you already know that WANT harbors fear and other negativity. It is better to substitute WANT with ALLOWING.

Lester taught that all human desires could be classified under three basic categories:

Wanting to Control (WC) circumstances, people, events, things, relationships, mind, etc.

Wanting Approval (WA) from some higher power and others; wanting our own approval and wanting to approve/disapprove others.

Wanting Security (WS), wanting to be safe.

Negative emotions can be divided into six basic categories: Apathy, Grief, Fear, Lust, Anger and Pride (**AGFLAP**). Each of the six categories harbor many other related emotions.

Anger, for example, may be expressed as Irritation, Annoyance, Disgust, Disturbance, Violence, Willfulness, etc.

The goal is to move from AGFLAP into a state of Courageousness, Acceptance and Peace (**CAP**).

Courageousness. On the scale of action, Lester describes it as a willingness to go into action without fear, to give, to correct, to change whatever needs it, the willingness to let go, to move on.

Acceptance. Get the feeling: everything is OK just the way it is. On the scale of action, Lester describes it as no need to change anything. No judgment of good or bad. It's just is... It is beautiful as it is, and it's OK the way it is. It is wonderful out there... I am enjoying everything as it is.

Peace. On the scale of action, Lester describes it as I am, I am whole, complete, totally into my Self. Everyone and everything is part of myself. It's all perfect.

Before releasing bring yourself in one of these states by imagining the end result, because only in these states releasing is effective; then we continue releasing until we become peaceful and loving regarding the subject of releasing. Peace and love are not an emotion, but an emotionless, thoughtless, natural state of your nature, your Self. Peace is synonymous with life, beingness and harmony with nature. It is superior and far more beneficial than any emotional state, because it takes one beyond the influence of the subconscious mind. It is the most natural state of being and qualifier of our spiritual progress. The inner state of unbroken, unencumbered peace is Freedom.

Every human emotion or feeling can be identified as Wanting Control, Wanting Approval or Wanting to be safe and secure. Quite often these wants may overlap, which is all right; just choose the WANT you feel is most appropriate for the moment.

Let's say you are in a state of "apathy." You feel unwanted; you have no interest and no energy... Is it WC or WA? Want of Approval would probably be more appropriate here. Or if you are disgusted with someone who lied to you, you are "angry." Anger is WANT of Control.

Although wants are not feelings, they definitely have a "feel" to them. Wanting Approval has a kind of "gimme" feeling to it—a kind of soft neediness. Wanting Control has a hardier feeling. It is more pushy and assertive. Wanting to be safe always has fear in it.

Remember that WANT is a lack. Nothing is wrong with giving or receiving approval or being in control. It is not the actual state that limits us, but the WANTING of it. Releasing WANTS is more effective than releasing a singular emotion. When you let go of WANT you are letting go of a piece of every feeling that may be stored under this kind of WANT of approval, control or security. Pain and misery come from WANTING Approval, Security and Control. Wanting approval, to be safe or to be in control is another way of saying we want to be loved. All joy comes from giving approval and giving up WANTING to control, it comes from inner knowledge that safety is our natural state, which is a way of giving Love.

Give yourself approval as often as you can. Give it for no reason—just because you Love yourself, because you are alive, because it's great to be in this world and because you're born to succeed. Accepting yourself completely as you are now and unconditionally loving yourself is first step on the path of realization.

Smiles and laughter are great releasing tools and as helpful as giving yourself approval. No other animal, only man has this really amazing ability to laugh. An innate human ability, laughter has spiritual quality to it. The more aware you become, the more you will smile at yourself and the absurdity of the life you used to live unaware, at the others, who you now Love although they continue to fall into absurdity.

Unknowingly, Christianity made Jesus look very sad. Images of Jesus don't reflect happiness that is always present in images of Indian Krishna, in them there is no laughter of Lao Tzu. Jesus should be shown laughing, because he was a down to earth human being. He loved good company, he enjoyed being with people. He was Jewish and Jews have best jokes about themselves and others. The New Testament was written 300 years after Jesus' death, so the publishers did whatever they pleased. They edited out Jesus' jokes, his teaching of happiness.

Sit down in a reclining chair, relax and smile. No reason is necessary, simply make yourself smile and watch. Keep smiling with your eyes half closed and you would notice your all body relaxing, smiling. Then become very serious for a moment and take a note of immediate change: your body is not relaxing any longer, but becoming tenser, the more serious you become. A smile is magic. It relaxes you, and it also affects everyone around you. Seeing you smiling people ease up, cheer up, begin to smile. But your smile must be genuine even when it has no reason behind it. Actually no reason is necessary, for a smile is simply a natural celebration of life.

Become a smiling billionaire. As you practice this natural gift you may realize that even healing is possible with a smile, because as body is getting more relaxed, it takes care of fixing itself. Smile needs to become a part of your nature, engraved in your subconscious mind.

Once I met a man called Wolfi. He was 43 and a German. Handsome and strong, Wolfi was always wearing an irresistible smile. His smile was so natural, I couldn't imagine him without it. Wolfi owned a bicycle shop in a small German town and was making enough money, for him and his girlfriend to travel every winter all over the world. The secret was Wolfi's personality, expressed in his sincere charming open smile. To my question about his business success, Wolfi said simply: "I am very friendly." Indeed, his smile betrayed this truth.

Irisha, my ex-wife was another example. Whenever I saw her, a warm engaging smile was always playing on her lips. When she came to America she knew no English, had no education. But only a few years later, she became a computer program tester, starting with $35,000 salary. In two years she was making 55K and then 80K. A better half of Irisha's success was due to her soft, friendly personality expressed in an appealing natural smile. One employer even said that she is hired because of 50% of her knowledge and 50% of her charming personality.

AGFLAP pulls us into the past or future. Releasing can happen only in the present. Like meditation, releasing will keep you in the present because it takes place only in the present. Though to be aware in the present is incomparably better state than the one of past memories or indulgence in the future, keep in mind that fleeting moment of the present is also a concept, so don't be attached to it. When free from the influence of all concepts you will forever experience this fleeting moment for what it is—eternity.

I would like to reiterate that releasing will be effective only when we are releasing, being in the state of either

Courageousness, Acceptance or Peace. The entire process of releasing must be always done lovingly. Therefore before starting the releasing bring yourself into one of the states of CAP with loving attitude. It is easily done when you imagine the end result of a particular releasing: wonderful relationship, money in your account, new house, whatever you are releasing on. Remember to start with accepting and loving yourself unconditionally.

The process of Releasing consists of five steps:

1. Become aware of the emotion and lovingly accept it.
2. Feel the emotion somewhere in the body. Anger for example is often felt in the pit of the stomach or in the chest. Find that spot and feel your anger there. It won't take too long before you notice that the more you concentrate on your anger, the weaker it becomes. This happens, because instead of "feeding" it with your energy, you are withdrawing the energy by calmly witnessing your emotion.
3. Identify the emotion as Wanting Approval (WA) or Wanting Control (WC).
4. Relax into the emotion
5. Release the emotion. As you keep your attention on it, let it go by asking

- Could I let it go?   Yes!

- Would I let it go?   Yes!

- When?   Now!

Inhale, while asking the last question. Then open an imaginary window in the spot where you feel the

63

emotion, and with exhalation, let the energy flow freely out of that window, while saying "Now!" Imagine bluish, almost transparent energy flowing out.

A feeling or emotion is nothing but energy; it is neither "bad" nor "good." We give it different names in order to relate it to different mental states.

The energy flows out... It is gone! Still, ask yourself:

And More?... Answer: Yes! And let more of it to flow out...
And More?... Yes! And let even more of it out...
And even More?... Yes! Let more of it out...
And even More?... Yes! Let more of it out...
And even More?... Yea! Let more of it out...

Try to feel the feeling again. Imagine situation that made you feel angry. It would help you to locate more anger within you.

Keep repeating the process until you find yourself out of AGFLAP and in CAP (Courageousness Acceptance and Peace).

It is important to continue releasing until you are at peace. It may take time, but time thus spent is ten times worth the effort. You will find that nothing is more rewarding than your state of peace.

There should be no thinking or analyzing. You must say "yes" regardless of how you feel about it. When your attachment to a feeling that you're releasing is strong, it may be hard to say "yes." But, if you won't listen to your mind, you would say "yes" regardless of how you feel.

***

It is good to know that we don't need to change anything except our capacity to love. When there is a problem we need to love more and problems disappear, says Lester. When our Love is total, all problems disappear. Releasing helps to witness one's thinking all the time. Because awareness is witnessing and it doesn't employ mind, when you practice releasing, your mind will soon begin losing its dominant position, like in meditation, and will start obeying your command.

The mind is a two-edged sword: with the edge of ignorance you can easily decapitate yourself, the edge of wisdom, which is Awareness and Love can set you free. Releasing is also a two-edge sword, with both edges helping you to happiness. When you accept a feeling as your own and witness it, the feeling will lose its strength, but your witnessing and accepting must be total. When you let go of wanting to control a feeling, it too, will be gone, but your decision to let it go must be unwavering.

Awareness is our own light. When this light begins to shine, darkness of ignorance disappears of itself. Darkness has no substance. It is nothing but absence of light, and absence and presence cannot coexist. Awareness and AGFLAP cannot co-exist. Try to be aware and angry at the same time—it is impossible: you are either aware or angry; if you are overwhelmed with grief, lust or pride, you are not aware, but driven by these feelings.

Awareness is Love, which is an 'extension' of *Pure Awareness* into the human world, the proven solution to every problem. Greed enslaves those who are not aware of their own light. They forgot they were born emperors, and live in spiritual poverty of messy lives. It is impossible to become greedy when you know that all treasures of the universe are within you. One who is always aware knows that he is wealthy and has all he needs when he needs it.

Anger is nothing but wounded ego. One who is aware knows that ego is but illusion, a trick of the mind and is not real: it simply doesn't exist. Something that doesn't exist cannot be wounded.

Emotions stored within, are layered on top of one another like tissues in a box. You don't remember when or how most of them got there. Negative and positive, their number is countless. Let go of one, and another immediately takes its place. Do your best to release all of them, so that energy may flow freely.

In the course of this practice, you may experience more negative feelings than before. It feels this way because, by tapping into your subconscious, you are exposing what was hidden from view. As you progress, you will begin to feel lighter, less moody, less bothered by your feelings. Their influence will become weaker. When you release a significant part of your emotional "archive," the rest of it may disappear as if by itself. You will still have feelings, but they won't affect you nearly as much as before; you will get into a habit of releasing them immediately, effortlessly.

In the process of releasing, our suppressed energy is literally released. When energy is no longer locked within, it will rejuvenate, enabling us to fly instead of crawl.

Peace is a state in which everything and everyone is accepted the way they are. Such acceptance is only possible when we are in love with the entire universe. This also means unconditional acceptance of yourself. Such a Love doesn't mean you will approve corruption, lies, violence and people expressing this negativity, but you will bear no malice, because you know that it is but expression of ignorance which is not real, because, as Jesus said, people don't know what they do. This negativity will not disturb your state of calm.

Your mind would try to convince you otherwise, it would tell you that corruption is real that people get caught and put in prison for taking bribes; people die in wars, and this is reality, and you must hate those who start wars. Nevertheless, when you become Awareness and Love, there will be no negativity left in you. When you're facing or dealing with the negativity expressed by others, you will instantly release negative feelings that may rise, if some of it is still left in you, and act as an impartial witness. No longer driven by emotions, you will see clearly and know instantly what needs to be done.

The state of loving peace is the only appropriate state to be in. If you're not peaceful, find out what is it within you that deprives you of peace and let it go. Keep letting go until your state of peace is restored.

The feeling of aversion, repulsion is a negative feeling. Also, the feeling of attachment to anyone or anything is negative and, therefore is as damaging as anger or jealousy, because it blinds, enslaves, shuts off reason and blocks your intuitive channel. Having relationships and having things is far more enjoyable when there is no attachment.

A feeling of superiority is as negative as fear. When you feel someone is superior, somewhere deep within you will detect a feeling of inferiority. Get rid of both. Oneness and harmony are natural qualities of every human being and at some point in life everyone feels it. All existence needs to be respected, not just for its sake, but for our own sake. The idea of superior or inferior was created by an imperfect society. The Pope is not superior to anyone in his flock; an elementary school teacher is not inferior to the president of the country. Every human being is a "sleeping" Self, dreaming a dream of life. It is that simple: a teacher is dreaming his dream, president – his. Unlike unaware humanity, Awareness knows neither superiority nor inferiority.

And here comes Pride, a well camouflaged negativity that makes you feel superior to someone or something else—an unmistakable sign of low awareness. 'Pride goes before a fall.' This folk saying is a reminder of what to expect as result of being proud.

There is no standing still. If one doesn't move forward he is moving backward. If he is stirring his life in the direction of the world, he is moving away from home, away from Self, because the world is but a bundle of limitations. However, the closer we are to the Center, the more we enjoy the world of harmony and oneness.

We need to take full responsibility for what is happening to us. Get into the habit of bringing hidden causes up into mind, so that you can drop it and be free of it.

When something unpleasant happens to you, ask yourself, "What did I do to cause this?" The answer will come up. Evaluate the cause, love it, and let it go.

It is only to our benefit to reverse everything we said or did that was negative. Reverse it by letting go of the associated negative emotions and changing them to Love. Reverse the negatives each time you encounter it. The mind feeds on negativity; the more negativity the mind absorbs, the more alive it feels. Mind believes it is a king —wary king about trying new things. It is always worried and releasing worry makes it worry even more, because the last thing it would want to risk even in face of death, is control over You (it is a capital Y in order to distinguish the real You— Awareness—from Your mind and body). Releasing helps to end the mind's domination and mind senses it. It and will try all it can to prevent you from releasing. This is Resistance, the best friend of apathy, grief and fear. Resistance is also on good terms with lust, anger and pride—the whole bouquet of AGFLAP. Resistance is a major block to releasing—it 'corks' the negativity within your body. Your loving and firm decision to be free from the influence of negative thoughts and emotions will allow you to let go of Resistance.

∗∗∗

If awareness is the mother of fortune, diligence is its sister. Your happiness will always be proportionate to your awareness, your capacity to Love, which means it will be proportionate to your releasing negativity that includes Resistance. Lester sighted some colorful samples of resistance:

– Wanting to control another person, whom you think is trying to control you, you can only experience your own resistance.

– The "I can't" is resistance. It takes a decision to keep releasing despite the habit of holding down the feelings.

– Resistance is when you haven't decided yet whether to do a thing or not. You are doing it anyway and it is difficult.

– Resistance – is pushing against the world so that it will push back.

If there were no resistance, you will be free from negativity very quickly. You constantly have to release the resistance in order to let the feelings up and out.

When we have no *Resistance*, no *Fear* and no *Wants*, when we don't wish to change anything but accept everything the way it is, we are free.

Resistance is a negative program that we unconsciously created in order to protect all other negative programs, which together constitute our illusory ego. Ego is made of limitations, superimposed on Mind. Ego is ignorance, it thrives on negativity. As a matter of fact the more negativity it devours the more energetic it seems to become: the illusory ego asserts itself by living as exciting as possible. It loves risk, car racing, horse racing, any kind of racing, parachuting, gliding, competitive sports, and so on. The more dangerous is undertaking, the more ego (mind) gets excited, the more alive it becomes. Mountain climbing, deep water diving, solo ocean crossing, boxing, etc. get ego even more excited with danger. Ego feels even more alive with wars, genocides, conquests, arguing, fighting, murder and so on and so forth. When we cannot do these things ourselves, we watch it live, and when this is not possible, we glue ourselves to our TV set and keep feeding our mind with negativity. We love to watch all sorts of dangers and disasters, feeling safe hiding in our chair. The problem is not in doing or watching. It lies in ignorant attachment, when participation and watching are done unaware.

Thus our limited, barely aware mind takes us away, as far as possible, from our home within. And the further we get from our home, the more miserable we become. *Resistance* protects all that garbage. It protects ego, for higher awareness means death of ego. If we try and explain this to an ego we face *Resistance*: the ego of the listener gets angry, it starts an argument and comes up with many words 'validating' the Mind's limitations, justifying negative thoughts and emotions and downgrading Awareness: 'No one! I mean no one tells me what to do!' shouts ego. Of course, this is a lie, as everything of the ego is a lie, as ego itself is lie. Your mind—ego—always tells you what to do and you are forever obeying it. This is why you have a life of misery and only glimpses of happiness.

Ignorance *Resists,* wisdom accepts.

To live life of happiness, we must open and nourish our ability to accept and love, let go of *Resistance*, and become one with all that exists, including all concepts and ideas of humanity, including people's egos. There should be no exceptions.

It may sound like a contradiction. But let us take closer look at *Resistance*, for example, in relation to illness. When we get ill, we immediately begin to *Resist* our state of illness and disapprove it along with our body, for getting ill. Mind loves disapproving. When we *Resist* illness, the illness doesn't care... but our mind and body suffer, because *Resistance* creates tension in the mind and tense mind stiffens the body. When body is tense, its natural functions, including immune system, begin to malfunction in proportion to the degree of the tension. The result is obvious.

Actually our immune system never fights disease. Under normal relaxed circumstances it would absorb bacteria or virus' and let the body eliminate them. It is functioning like computer's antivirus program that catches virus', deposits them into a volt and deletes them. When we are free of *Resistance* we won't even notice when some deadly virus have entered our body and is thrown out. When there is no *Resistance* our involvement is totally unnecessary. It is never necessary; we make it look necessary when we are under spell of ignorance, when we are barely aware. If we are getting ill, it means there is *Resistance* somewhere, there is tension and stress. When it happens, let's welcome illness and see what follows. By the act of welcoming we acknowledge that we abandoned *Resistance* and have no fear of illness. Now let us lovingly let go of illness. As we keep letting it go, our mind is getting more relaxed. Consequently our body is also getting more relaxed, and all its systems resume their normal function. Result is obvious: sooner recovery.

We need to *Resist* nothing, but accept everything. If there is something out there you want to change, adjust your attitude towards it to a loving attitude and love more. But first, remember to love yourself. Loving yourself will not make you feel superior; loving yourself dissolves ego, loving yourself makes you one with the universe, whose nature is Love.

When there is a problem we need to love more and the problem disappears. When our Love is total, all problems disappear at once.

Fear is a hidden source of all other negative emotions; it is rooted in a *fear* of death. We don't pay attention to this fact, because who is interested in death while alive? No one, except those who work in cemeteries, morgues and funeral parlors. And even they are not interested in a matter of their own death, because death is always happening to someone else. Having such disturbing jobs—a natural trigger of *fear*—they run away from their *fear*, doing their best to never face it. But *fear* is dangerous because it tends to pull toward what we *fear*.

Somewhere deep inside we know, and rightly so, that we can never die. But we don't want to think about death; we would rather watch TV or get involved into an empty chat on a kind of social substitute for an idiot box. My friend Charles came up with a good name for Facebook and its like: "Social masturbation networks". Thus, we neither wish to explore origins of fear nor deal with our *fears*. Subconsciously, we push our fears deep into subconscious, where they are hard to find. There it germinates and then produces unwanted results.

In 1943, through my realizations, I lost all fear. How nice that is! Says Lester in his Autobiography.

Fear loves our *wants*, because it hides right behind want. Let's say we have a goal to win a few million dollars in a lottery. Some people actually do win millions. Unfortunately only one out of ten winners benefits out of it. Why not me? So we have this goal: I want to win $15 million. Now look carefully behind that want. What do you see there? A bouquet of negativity: doubts, uncertainty, suspicion, a lack of confidence, and of course, *fear* that you will not get your millions. How this *fear* helps toward your goal is more than obvious: it sabotages it, making sure you never get anything, and never reach any goal.

At the same time, we know some people who are openly fearful about their goal, nevertheless reach their target. Another contradiction? Not at all. Like to everything, there is a reason for this seeming contradiction. These people may look *fearful* outwardly, but they are doubtless and *fearless* inwardly. And subconscious feelings are stronger than conscious feelings. Outwardly nice and kind people may be inwardly fearful, lacking self-confidence, lacking determination and thus living in need. Like any other negative emotion, *fear* must be detected, welcomed and lovingly let go.

Lester Levenson was extremely fearful of death, but his decision to live was more powerful than fear of death. Once he made this decision, his self-confidence grew sky high, his determination became supremely intense and he stumbled upon happiness and Freedom in three short months. He knew nothing about Freedom; he was actually looking for true happiness with no sorrow. And Freedom happened as if by accident. But Freedom cannot happen any other way except 'as if by accident'. However, there is no accident at becoming free. There is always tremendous intensity and great determination involved. Lester also proved that it is possible to become free in no time. What is three months? Anyone can isolate himself for three months if he is absolutely determined to be free.

But we always find reason to postpone this final and only step. Why? Because we commit ourselves to other things, and though we are very interested in Freedom, we are really not determined, we are afraid to let go of our garbage, we are reluctant to make this decision, we would rather keep searching all of our life, keep meditating and studying teaching. It feels nice, and it gives us comfort and satisfaction: Oh yes, I am meditating, I am improving myself, I even have many gains through releasing; it is such a wonderful thing... releasing! But we don't get the most important, priceless gain of awakening. If you want to be free, make this final decision now. Not tomorrow, but now!

Advanced Releasing Exercise [11]

Pure Mind or Awareness forever is an absolute clarity... within us, it is merged with love. It is our Self, with no limitations...

Let us start with letting go of whatever we are feeling right now and move into Courageousness, Acceptance and Peace.

We begin with Courageousness. It's a wonderful place, where we are willing to do whatever it takes, no matter what: a place of absolute willingness to do anything. We are adventurous, alive, powerful, self-sufficient and secure. We have a vast vision. We have been here before in this wonderful place and can access it from our past memory, when we were in trouble. We are here right now.

---

[11] Courtesy of Steve Winn, wwwReleaseTechnique.com

On the scale of action, Lester says, 'Courageousness is a willingness to go into action without fear, to give, to correct, to change whatever needs it, the willingness to let go, to move on.' It is a very distinct state. Notice how you are immediately becoming more aware, as you move into this state.

And from here, let's move into Acceptance. Just a shift, a different way of a being expressing itself: Acceptance. Get the feeling: everything is OK just the way it is. On the scale of action, Lester says, 'No need to change anything. No judgment of good or bad. It just is... It is beautiful just as it is, and it's OK just the way it is. It is wonderful out there... I am enjoying everything just as it is.

So take a look, wherever you are, sitting, driving, whatever it is that you're doing. Can you allow it to be beautiful just as it is? Can you allow yourself to enjoy your surroundings, which includes your body, just as it is? Can you love your body just as it is? The room you are in, just as it is? The city you are in, just as it is? And will it be OK with you to make the decision, and it is just a decision, to feel about wherever you are in life, being just beautiful?

Well, the mind may check on this and that, and yet, it is all Awareness, Beingness, and it is always beautiful. Other words Lester used to describe this: fullness, gentle, glowing, gracious, harmonious. And again, notice where you are right now. What it feels like. Be aware. Contrast it to the state of Courageousness... There is a cool air about this state of Acceptance. When you notice the differences between the two states it will allow you to access this state of Awareness more freely.

From this place of Acceptance, where everything is OK the way it is, allow yourself to move to a state of Peace. On a scale of action, Lester describes it as I am, I am whole, complete, totally into my Self. Everyone and everything is part of my Self. It's all perfect.

Whatever you're now feeling, whatever you're experiencing... can you let it go and let it be even more perfect?

Would it be OK with you, if you dissolve the boundaries, whatever they are: boundary of your body, your house, your car, your property, boundary of your country... Can you dissolve these boundaries, and allow everything to be seen as your Self, your own Beingness, Awareness. Immediately, everything becomes quiet, even more serene, more still.

Would it be OK with you if you live in peace every day, all day?

Would it be OK with you, if everyone you've met will be radiantly peaceful beings, a part of you, of your own Self? If everyone is seen in total serenity, total peace, the world is automatically becoming peaceful and serene. Other words to describe this: stillness, kindness, tranquility, unlimited, whole.

And check to see if our friend the mind has been active lately, trying to figure things out. Can you let go of trying to figure it out? Mind always has a list of favorite things it is trying to figure out. Could you let that process go and allow yourself just be and rest in Awareness? Let us ask the mind if it knows the solution of whatever you're trying to figure out. Of course it doesn't. It is one of the most pointless exercises in our lives, to keep asking the mind for an answer, when it doesn't have an answer. And when we do this, it comes back at us with a judgment. It says, 'beat yourself up! Is there something wrong with you? There we go again: asking me about something I don't know!' Is that helping us to get the solution? What it does... it keeps us on the surface of our mind: all that asking, beating ourselves up.

So now we have a decision to make. Are we going to keep being negative, beating ourselves up, standing on the surface of our mind? Or, do we want to let that go and move into productivity, quietness and deepness? Of course, we want to be quieter and deeper.

Then, can you let go of disapproving of yourself for whatever reason? And let it go some more, and even more... Still more. And what is that situation that needs resolving? Would you let go disapproving of that? And more, and more, and more. And instead of disapproving of yourself, will you just be gracious and magnanimous, loving and kind with the situation, allowing it to be without any judgment? Give it love and approval, and see what happens. Give it some more love and approval, and more, and more. And give yourself some love and approval, and more. And give yourself even more love and approval, and even more, and more. Awareness... give Awareness love and approval. Give your ego love and approval.

Every time we give love and approval, we get higher and higher, quieter and quieter. Check your mind right now, check your body. You'll notice if you feel lighter, quieter, easier. It is almost a mathematical process, a mathematical equation: every time we give ourselves love and approval, we feel lighter, quieter, easier.

From this state of wholeness look at your life and see if there is any part that you're resisting. Anything in your life that frustrates you, irritates you that you try to exclude from your wholeness? See if there is any question, any sensation about that. And just kinesthetically (instantly) let that energy go. Let it go some more..., and more... And will it be OK with you, if you reclaim that part of your life in terms of yourself? We are responsible for our pictures: everything that we picture is part of ourselves.

When you give yourself love and approval, when you let go of disapproving yourself, the mind is automatically quieter. You know a peace of mind. What is it worth to you, that peace of mind? Is it worth releasing? Is it worth of keeping your momentum up? What is more important than fully establishing peace of mind? Ask your heart, what is more important? Doesn't everything in life get better, when you know a peace of mind, when you have a quieter mind?

Why waste your time and resources? Why not keep to the fort and along with it the entire kingdom. As Jesus said: Seek you first the kingdom of heaven, and everything else will be given unto you... If you capture peace of mind, everything else comes. Everyone will want to do business with you, hire you, whatever it is. Everyone will want to be with you when you have peace of mind. What is it worth to you? Would it be OK with you if you make a decision? Irrevocable decision that says I am going for freedom, no matter what. Why not?

Some times when we make a decision like that, thoughts come up? What comes up? Check and see if you are wanting approval, wanting control, or wanting to be safe and secure. If you are, can you let that go? And let it go some more... and more. And, again, could you make irrevocable commitment to freedom. No matter what comes up in your life, you're going for Freedom.

And again check, what fear, what resistance comes up, if there is any wanting approval, wanting control, wanting to be safe and secure. And if some of it is there, let all of the wanting go, all that lacking[12]... go.

Now, let's see if there is any resistance in your life... When we go to CAP, and back to apathy, and again, to CAP, and then—to fear. And what about liking to be in CAP, and not liking to be down in AGFLAP? That's an

---

[12] Want is lack

aversion. Check and see if you have any aversion to your AGFLAP. The easiest way to check it is to see if there are people out there, in the state of AGFLAP that you don't like. Let's say, you don't like apathetic people. That's an aversion. I don't like people who are fearful. It's an aversion. And... could you see this AGFLAP go back into peace, go back into Awareness, into wholeness, and will you embrace this AGFLAP and love it? And let it go.

Get a picture of your AGFLAP, whatever it looks like to you. May be it gives you emotional disturbance. And could you embrace that in a wholeness of peace—to make completeness of peace. Will you embrace it, love it, and let it go again.

Let the whole picture dissolve.

Check if you have been judging yourself rather than an AGFLAP. And again, go to peace and let yourself love the judgment... and let it go.

What's going well in your life, what are some of your gains and victories? Can you go to a place of gratitude for whatever is going well in our life, and just love it, appreciate it, praise it, be thankful for it.

Will it be OK with you if you made the decision to go free, this year and see if resistance comes up? Some say, it's too much; it's too fast. I have too much of an AGFLAP, this and that... Can you see that just as a thought and let it go?

Lester went "home free" in three short months... For you, it also can be a simple entrance into peace. Identify with Awareness, Beingness—just be. When something comes up, you let it go. Something comes up, you let it go. Therefore in peace, aren't we free?

Check if you have any resistance about going free this year. What doubts do you have about this? Some think it is a little too quick. Some say, it takes a lifetime to do. However, there are people who drop their ego just like that. You may say, wait a second, they dropped their ego, and the stuff comes back later. So what? They dropped their ego and they are transformed.

Would it be OK with you, if you've forged your intention today to be free? And if you fall out of it a later, so what? For the day, at least, will you let yourself reside in acceptance and peace? Don't worry about the future. Don't worry if it lasts or doesn't last. Just for the day, allow yourself to be whole, complete, quiet, and if something comes up, you just let it go. As long as you're letting it all go, isn't there at least a degree of freedom? Whatever comes up, we let it go. When we have a quiet peaceful mind, it doesn't matter what comes up in our life.

Set your intention for the day. Let yourself see that day unfolding. Let's get a picture of that day, the most perfect day of freedom. What it looks like? What it feels like? Where are you going? It looks like you're going somewhere as if you would if you weren't free; you're talking to people as you would if you weren't free. And then—aha! I've allowed myself to be free—quiet, peaceful, when I do all these things in my life.

See this picture, be in love with this picture, give gratitude to this picture for your day of complete Freedom. Thank you, Awareness, for things so clear, for such clarity. I just love this. Go today, with that clarity, with that lovingness... with that freedom.

Let the picture come up and see what is in the way of it. A perfectly free day. Whatever comes up, whatever wanting comes up... just let it go... and more... and more... and even still more... and have the most free day imaginable, filled with love and clarity.

Spontaneous Irrevocable Decision and mind Control

For in and out, above, about, below,
This nothing but a magic Shadow-show
Played in the box whose candle is the Sun,
Round which we phantom figures come and go.

Mind is a sophisticated biological computer. It is a computer of our own making. Very powerful, this computer can either destroy our life or make it a wonderful experience. Our own ignorance is preventing us from recognizing this simple fact: whatever we willingly or unknowingly download into this computer will affect our life. At this very moment this computer is running your life. You think you are in control but you are not; your mind-computer is in control. The following examples show how little control we really have.

I was driving quite fast. Suddenly a policeman appeared and motioned me to pull over. I pushed the brakes, but the car won't stop! At this very moment I woke up. I was practicing releasing for a quite some time and learned to pay careful attention to premonitions. As a general rule, when one wakes up because of a dream, it must be a warning signal.

I was an extremely careful driver that day. At 4.45 p.m. I was driving East on Olympic Blvd. As I was approaching a traffic signal, it changed to yellow. "All right," I thought, "it is still enough time to cross," and I entered an intersection. There was a flash from an automatic camera hanged high up on the pole, resulting in $350 fine plus a day in a Traffic school.

It is extremely difficult to override a program that is already running in our mind even when we are warned. But, it is possible to get rid of the potential effect by letting go of the cause as soon as it is created or whenever we remember about it. Unfortunately, we quickly forget about causes we originate. Contemplating the reason for this incident, I remembered that on several occasions I was afraid of being caught running the yellow/red light. Had I been more aware of my thoughts and feelings and let go of impatience and fear, I would have eliminated the cause and the result (or effect) would never have come to pass.

Unless we clearly understand how mind works, we must get into the practice of continuing releasing for, if we always do what we always did, we will always get what we've always gotten. Enough is enough! Let's make an Irrevocable Decision to Love ourselves and to release the blocks to happiness.

In the beginning of the Russian Perestroika, Nick Navarro, then famous Sheriff in Fort Lauderdale, Florida asked me to help him to invite a group of Russian police officers as his guests. At the end of this unusual gathering I was awarded an Honorable Police Deputy Badge. Smiling, Nick suggested that I keep my drivers' license together with the badge. He explained that if the Police officer asks for my driver's license, he will notice the badge, which could be quite helpful.

In my mind, I've occasionally played this scene. Then the whole thing went into an obscurity. Several years later my wife Irisha and I took a ride to visit our daughter in Santa Cruz University. Freeway was free of cars and Irisha wanted me to drive faster. Few minutes later I was stopped for speeding. Irisha said that my hand shook when I was pulling out the badge with my driver's license inside, but the rest of the incident was exactly as I had envisioned it. It was even funny. The officer asked to see the badge, inquired who I was working for and let us go.

I have a number of similar experiences on the record.

Once, I was madly in love with a beautiful actress. We decided to move in together. Early morning of that "moving" day I woke up from a loud voice ringing in my head: "Don't do it!" The voice was very convincing, I instantly felt that my "moving" plan was doomed, but I had no power to make a change. We moved in together. The very next day I moved out.

It was my last year in the Navy Academy in St. Petersburg, Soviet Union. At about 4 o'clock in the morning I was called to my last 4-hour duty shift. As my consciousness was slowly returning to me I suddenly heard a voice ringing loudly in my head: "You are wasting your life here. Walk out!" The voice was very real. I obeyed the command. My friends and my mother were advising me against leaving. It seemed to be so wrong to through away six years of study and a career as an engineer and navy officer. Eleven years later I've forever left my homeland where I spent 33 years of my life. My classmates all ended up serving in the Northern Fleet's nuclear facilities.

Why was I able to follow this inner advice? Decision! It was Spontaneous Irrevocable Decision that 'walked me out' of the school. The message was intuitive and my decision was intuitive as well. I didn't think, didn't analyze situation, I didn't do anything, except spontaneously making a decision that was as intuitive as a message. It was effortless. I made it at the time I received a message, and it was final. For a while I even forgot the whole thing, until I had to go to the hospital with appendicitis. There I remembered about my decision and asked my very young and beautiful lady-doctor to get me out of the academy. And she did. After I met Lester, I learned more about an utmost importance of the decision, of an irrevocable decision. Such a decision functions as releasing. It has tremendous power, because it banishes everything at once, which stands in the way of the goal: Fear, Resistance and Want. It just kills this three-headed serpent and inexplicably creates circumstances necessary to accomplish the goal. Though it was nearly impossible for a young man to leave any military institution in the Soviet Russia, fortune smiled on me and I was out in two months. Except for the appendicitis, my leaving was smooth, even a pleasant venture.

Even today I ponder on this impeccable mechanism of irrevocable decision. It works like a clock.

Looking back, I remember another situation that proved once more an incredible power of the Decision. I didn't plan to leave USSR. Once, my friend Jacob, at the time head of financial department of the ministry of film, told me how easy I could leave for Israel. In three months I was out. Many people struggle for years waiting for permission to leave. I made an Irrevocable Decision and was out in no time. There were helpful circumstances however: I knew little to nothing about the struggle of others and had no fear of refusal or persecution. I had no fear and no doubts, and my decision was irrevocable. In the chapter *Goals* there is example of how Lester demonstrated it even better with decisions he made after he went free.

I was ignorant, and I was not sure at the time of how to make those decisions, which proves that even being not yet free, we have this ability to make decisions spontaneously and irrevocably, the decisions that work miracles. Today I know that the main reason for success of Irrevocable Decision is intuitive spontaneity that instantly releases all related negativity. It is the instant releasing of all emotions and thoughts: negative and positive. But how irrevocable decision actually does it, how is it able to banish all those thoughts and emotions at once, what mechanism it employs, remains a great puzzle, a releasing miracle of the Irrevocable Decision.

Irrevocable decision is made without any concern for the future. We don't have any idea of what will happen then. Miraculously, everything happens in the best way, it happens perfectly, beyond our wildest dreams. When I left the navy academy, my friend mentioned Moscow film school, which I had never heard of before, and I loved making pictures. Despite very high competition and having no time to get prepared for exams, I was accepted and film making happened to be my calling.

I left Russia with a three-month-old son, wife and $100 in my pocket(well, there were also three suitcases). However, life in Israel was wonderful; it was good in Canada and the U.S.

The following is an example of another irrevocable decision. For more than 10 years I was an owner of R Ranch in the Sequoia National Forest. The beautiful Sierra Mountains reminded me of Eastern Siberia, Russia, where I traveled many years ago. Once I stopped to watch colorful sunset in the Sequoias. The sun just rolled down beyond the Great Sierra Range outlining its snow covered peaks with a reddish glow flashing against darkened blue skies. "I must live here," I said to myself resolutely, "This is my home!" That was an irrevocable decision, made consciously with awareness and Love. It was also spontaneous. Driving by remote road several weeks later I saw a gate about 15 miles north of the Ranch. It was tall well-made cowboy gate. Everything about that place looked nice and peaceful and I left a note on the gate. Couple of weeks later I received a telephone call and came to the mountains again to meet the owners. Jim, a tall, strong, handsome man of about 45, and his beautiful wife Gloria showed me the place, which Jim has later named "Yuri's Hill... My dream was about to become a reality. But that was not all... Jim has actually managed the entire construction process. When about six months later I came back from Russia, there was a beautiful home standing solemnly on Yuri's Hill, overlooking aw-inspiring scenery. A grand valley was lying down below, as far as an eye could see, fortified on both sides by great mountains covered with large oaks and tall fur trees. "As inside, so is out," a thought crossed my mind, "Creation is perfect and understandable".

This is a recent example of the spontaneous Irrevocable Decision. I had to see a dentist to prepare four of my teeth for crowns. As I walked into a cozy office of Dr. Bob McCracken's, in Lake Isabella, I have spontaneously made an Irrevocable Decision to have no pain and use no anesthesia. When several moments later I listened to Doctor Bob, explaining to me why there should be crowns instead of fillings, and what is involved, I've found myself in a state similar to reverie. "If that's what you wish," said the Doctor, "then I would do my best to accommodate you. Are you sure you don't want Novocain?" As far as I was concerned, I was 100% okay without it.

Dr. Bob started to file my teeth—I felt no pain. When three teeth were done, Dr. Bob called in his staff to watch how the fourth tooth was prepared. He said that in more than 40 years of his practice, this is the first time when the patient wanted no anesthetic. He explained that 'shaving' a tooth under the gum, was painful procedure, and added that he is amazed to watch me showing no sign of pain.

To me however, there was nothing amazing about it. It felt natural, without tension and with no effort. There really was no pain, as we know it. However, when I felt some of it about to surface, I reminded pain: "Who is the boss here!" Then lovingly invite it to come up even more, and allow it to leave, disappear, evaporate. Of course, there was no effort, because effort is needed to overcome resistance and fear, to overcome negativity. Spontaneous Irrevocable Decision instantly banishes all negativity, together with resistance and fear.

I was not able to figure out exactly how Spontaneous Irrevocable Decision works, but realized that Spontaneous means intuitive. Intuition is voice of Awareness, our omnipotent, omniscient Self. When we are thoroughly released, and walk into a situation where Spontaneous Irrevocable Decision will be helpful, our Self 'sends' the necessary information to our mind. Actually, all information that we need in order to live happily is within us and is always available, but we are accessing it so rarely because of the never-ending buzz of the mind. When we are released, emotional-thinking process seizes along with subconscious' influence, the mind's limitations are no longer there, and information necessary for making Spontaneous Irrevocable Decision is immediately comprehended.

Ego hates pain. We resist it. Resistance creates tension. Tension is physical indication of something we don't want. However, 'want' harbors fear behind it, hidden in many 'what ifs'. We think "I want to make spontaneous Irrevocable Decision," and quickly adding: "But what if it won't work?" Also, if we 'want' to make spontaneous Irrevocable Decision, it is not spontaneous. All this means that in order to make Spontaneous Irrevocable Decision, we need to be released to a certain extent. Even though releasing mechanism is our natural possession, it works differently in different people, and most of us need to practice releasing. It is impossible to determine beforehand, how much releasing we need to do in order to reach this 'certain extent' threshold. It will only improve our lives, when we allow ourselves to be in the releasing mode all the time, instantly letting go of the negativity as it comes up. At some point, without giving it any thought, we will know that we know..., and will spontaneously make an Irrevocable Decision whenever it is necessary, and it will work miracles.

Spontaneity: what difference does it make? Spontaneous Irrevocable Decision can only be right, whereas not spontaneous Irrevocable Decision may be not a right decision; even when it is right, it still may be subject to doubts and fears. When spontaneous Irrevocable Decision "happens", we know, without saying, it is right, as well as there will be no doubts and fears. There may be some "ifs" lurking in the back of the mind, but like ripples upon the surface of deep quiet lake, they won't disturb our state of calm. One who is free, makes only spontaneous decisions, and all these decisions are irrevocable.

When I was about to leave Dr. Bob's office, receptionist Kate said that for a while my gums will feel sore. "No, they won't," I replied with a confidence of the one who knows that he knows, and I never felt any soreness.

It is usually others who suggest most of our minds' content, but it is we who are responsible for what is kept in our mind, because it is up to us to accept or reject what we are told. Unfortunately, we automatically accept many things. We don't know that such things like horror movies, news, expressions like "you are a pain in the neck", "I can't afford it" or "I am sick of this!" bad jokes, and much of other information will often become a part of our subconscious, silently influencing our decisions. If our mind is cleansed of all its content we will be in heaven and truly happy we will be free.

Our mind's programs consist of thousands of concepts, numberless tendencies, millions of thoughts. Continually adding information, these programs are haphazardly running our lives, more than often in a direction that is opposite to where we wanted to go. We know very little about our mind's programs because most of it is hidden in the subconscious. Releasing enables us to clean the mind and subconscious, thus letting our nature of Awareness and Love run our lives of true happiness.

***

In January I was in Tulum, Mexico, south of Cancun, making final changes to **the Gates of Dead.**

An endless beach of the sugar-white sand was soft, inviting with its virgin purity. Extended far into the shallow ocean, it seemed to mingle with languid emerald waves caressing its softly sloping shore.

A silvery seagull flew slowly along the shore, its wide spread wings almost motionless, hugging the warm air. It was followed by another. Playing with the gentle waves, the birds turned eastward, towards the horizon, where undulating streams of air made the sky and sea dissolve into each other. The seagulls flew higher and higher... and then disappeared, vanishing into the pale-blue nothingness of the sky.

It was midday, and the endless strip of beach was deserted. Then in the hazy distance, three human figures came alive, approaching. A little boy of about seven was moving effortlessly in a never-ending summersault routine; his body seemed to fly over land and sea. A tall handsome man and a beautiful young woman were following the boy, laughing, and playing, her long luxurious hair trailed freely in the wind.

They looked so happy.

I wanted to thank the boy for such a wonderful performance and the parents for having such a wonderful child, but suddenly they turned and were gone, lost in a maze of mangrove. I felt almost desperately that I want them to be always like this, always loving and happy, forever and ever and ever.

In the sky above the trees, pelicans flew on silent wings in perfect formation, riding freely with fair winds.

And I saw that the young family, the seagulls, and the pelicans, ocean, mangroves and palm trees, all nature around me, was but sheer happiness. I felt all that we need to be happy is to be in harmony with nature, with all life.

A tiny young woman walked freely by the water, splashing in it like a child. She was carrying a small board with hand-made jewelry pinned to it. Her bright yellow sari streamed in the wind, blending naturally with the white of the sand, the pale blue of the skies, and the light, almost transparent emerald of the lazy ocean waves.

She was 24 and a Russian, living in a beach cabana for almost a year, making jewelry and selling it to tourists.

"I love it here in Tulum," she said almost ruefully. At the end of March she would travel down south and later even further south. She decided she wanted to see much of the Americas this way, traveling from place to place, making a living with hand-made jewelry. She had no insurance, no savings and no fears.

"No money?" I asked.

She looked shyly up to my face. "I have enough," she said simply, and gave a sunny smile. Actually, she was wearing this gentle smile all the time; it was part of her nature, and it was bright and beautiful, like the beautiful jewelry she created.

I saw that she was happy and content. She made a decision, and she was in harmony with nature. The decision she made banished all doubts and fears, and being in harmony, she attracted happiness to her life.

And I saw that the life of harmony is always effortless, but man's mind is often tense. Mental tension requires effort, and effort is never in harmony with nature.

When there is no harmony, problems arise. Thus effort and tension are at the root of all human problems. Mental effort and tension are influenced by the negativity in thought and emotion. Once this influence is gone, tension and effort disappear, and problems are easily solved with clarity and Love.

Not all was well in the wonderland of Yucatan.

Greed and corruption were in a mortal clash with nature's harmony.

The land of the ancient Maya—with its unique underground water supply system delicately balanced by nature—is in great danger.

Cancun's flashy hotels, and the many small hotels along Tulum's beautiful beach, have no sewage system. Furtively, they are pumping all their waste down into natural caverns 300 feet deep, contaminating the ocean, creating a health hazard, and endangering the land's well-being.

And I saw that greed and anger is for those who never have enough.
Fear is for those who are afraid to lose.
Pride is for the fearful.
Ignorance is for the weak.
Love is for the strong at heart.

Man's well-being is rooted in harmony with nature, and the key to harmonious life is Love and Awareness[13].

---

[13] This little story is from *Gates of the Dead*, a novel by the author.

Clean-Up

Welcome to the special Clean-Up Process.

This short, easy to do, but remarkably helpful exercise will soon be among your favorite releasing tools.

On a regular basis, lovingly using Clean-Up will assist you to eliminate stress, maintain emotional balance, and expand the access to your inner world and to your creative functions. This process will also help you to integrate releasing into your daily life.

The great thing about Clean-Up is that you can do it almost anywhere and anytime. You can do it at work or at play, alone, or with those you love. Do it when you wake up, do it just before you go to sleep, do it any time when something comes up in your life that warrants it, but above all, do it because Clean-Ups are really wonderfully practical and a very powerful exercise. Like everything else, do it with love.

This Clean-Up text is created so it can be applied to any area of your life, professional or personal. You can use it again and again as a regular part of your releasing.

Sit back in your chair and get comfortable.

Just allow yourself to relax into the chair.

And let's view your day...

Could you sense any tension anywhere in your body, or any discomfort?

Concentrate on it.

Are you WANTING to change or control that feeling there? If so, can you let go of WANTING to change or control it? Just for this moment, would you? When?

And can you sense any more tension anywhere?Maybe tightness in your shoulder? And do you WANT to change or control that feeling?
If so, can you let go of WANTING to change or control that and just allow it to relax? Would you? When?

Let us go over your day…

Did you see, or speak with anyone today who stirred up some WANTING to control?
Could you let go of WANTING to control that person? Would you? When?
And if you think of them again, could you let go of WANTING to control them. If so, could you let go of WANTING to control that person?

Could you let go of WANTING to control them? Would you allow them to be different? Just to release? When?

Check it again. As you see that person, does it is stir up emotions of WANTING to control them?
Could you let go of WANTING to control that person? Would you? When?

Is there anything else that you are working on, that stirred up some WANTING control… Maybe a project, or work at home?

Could you let go of WANTING to control your project? Would you? When?

Would you just invite up that WANTING control? And could you just let it go, allowing yourself release just WANTING control and allow yourself to have it? Would you? When?

See if there is any WANTING of controlling an outcome, or the success of your project?

If so, could you let go of WANTING to control an outcome, or the success, just for this moment?

Are you sensing anything else you WANT to control in your life right now?

And whatever it is, could you let go of WANTING to control that?

Will you? When?

Is there anything about your releasing?

What about yourself personally that you WANT to change or control?

Can you let go of WANTING to change, or control that about yourself?

Will you? When?

Once again, is there something about yourself? Something you WANT to be different about yourself that you WANT to control in any way?

If so, can you let go of WANTING to control yourself just for this moment?

Will you? When?

Let's go a little deeper now. Did anything happened today that stirred some wanting of approval? And can you let go WANTING approval for that, or from that person? Will you? When?

Think about this situation again, or about that person. Can you invite more of that WANTING approval and WANTING that respect? Then can you let go WANTING it? Can you allow that WANTING approval just to release? Will you? When?

Can you think of someone in your world who stirs up WANTING approval? As you see them in your mind's eye, can you let go of WANTING their approval, just for this moment? Will you? When?

Can you sense anymore WANTING their respect, their approval or recognition in some way? And if so, can you let go of WANTING their approval and allow yourself to have it? Will you? When?

And if there is any project you have been working on recently that stirs some WANTING of approval from your colleagues or from the public? And if so, can you let go of WANTING approval for that project? Can you allow the lack of approval just to release?

Will you? When?

Once again, can you sense any more WANTING for that project, WANTING the acknowledgment and the respect for it? And if so, can you let go of WANTING approval and allow yourself to have it? Will you? When?

Can you sense any disapproval of yourself, or judging yourself right now? If so, could you let go of judging yourself, or disapproval of yourself, just for this moment? Would you? When? Can you invite up more of that? Is there anymore of that sense of judging yourself, or putting yourself down, or disapproving of yourself for something you might have done today or said?

Could you let go of disapproving, or judging of yourself just for this moment?

Would you? When?

If there is anything about your life that you are judging or disapproving of?

Could you let go judging that, or disapproving of that?Would you? When?

Is there anything about your releasing that stirs up some judgment or disapproval of yourself? Could you let go judging or disapproving of your ability to release? Would you? When?

Could you get yourself some approval right now, just for the heck of it? Would you? When?

And can you sense anymore of that disapproval? Could you just allow it to release and be replaced of acceptance of yourself? Just could you? Would you? When?

O.K. Let's go deeper still. Did anything happen today that stirred some WANTING to be safe and secure?Could you let go of wanting security and safety?

And when you think about that situation or that event, or maybe that person that stirred up that WANTING security, could you just allow that wanting security to release?

Would you? When?

Is there any project that you want security for, you want to be safe and be a success? And if so, could you let go of WANTING security for it and allow yourself to have it? Would you? When?

Can you see anything else in your life that stirs some wanting security? Maybe it is your health, relationship, or financial issue?   Would you just invite up that WANTING security?   Could you just let it go, allowing yourself release just WANTING security and allow yourself to have it? Would you? When?

If you think of your health, relationship, or finances again, or maybe there is a career issue, can you sense more of that WANTING to be safe and secure, of WANTING survival?   And could you let go of WANTING that and allow yourself to have it?

Check inside again.   Did anything happen today, anything in your business, or your home life, or your relationships in general that stirred up some WANTING to be safe and secure?   If so, could you let go of WANTING security? Would you? When?

And check inside again. Can you become aware of anymore WANTING security pushing out? If so, could you let go of WANTING security and allow yourself to have it? Would you? When?

Check inside if there are any WANTS stirred up in a moment. Maybe it is WANTING to control something, or WANTING approval, or some WANTING security?

And whichever want is stirred up, could you just allow it to release?

Once again, whichever WANT is stirred up now in a moment, be it some WANTING control, WANTING approval, or WANTING to be safe and secure... Whichever want it is, could you allow it to release? Would you? When?

In this quiet moment could you give yourself some approval for all the releasing you've done… and for your day? Could you just allow yourself some approval? Just for the heck of it?

Goals

You know that you are born to succeed. Whatever happened in the past should not be standing in the way of the present. It is you, who, through the law of cause and effect, which governs your life, made yourself to be punished. Make this law work for you so you will be only rewarded now and always. Turn your request to *Awareness* with Love, faith and confidence. It will take over, because your Self is all-powerful. Decree health, and *Awareness* will establish it, but relaxation is the key. You infer no opponent and you use no will power. Rest in the sense of deep conviction that this is done. Release all doubts. *Awareness* accepts the stronger of two contradictory propositions. Maintain this attitude of mind as true regardless of "evidence" to the contrary.

The error lies in our effort. Let it go. To use mental force is to presuppose that there is an opposition, but to believe is to accept something as true or live in the state of being it. As you sustain this mood, you shall experience the joy of achievement. Opposition is hiding within you in a form of negative thoughts and emotions that form blocks of tendencies and habits, preventing you from reaching your goal. There could be no outside opposition unless you created it within.

It is important to set goals and achieve them. We set and accomplish goals because we believe it will make us happy. Indeed it makes us happy, but only for a little while. Then happiness is gone, and we run away from ourselves with another goal. When life is almost gone we realize we were never happy and there is no happiness in site. Well, we said to ourselves, at least there were some moments of happiness... but we don't want to think how many times and how long these moment were, because there were only a few of them and they were incredibly short. Thus, unhappily, we unwillingly die, having no satisfaction, no happiness.

Society provokes us by examples of great accomplishments, great wealth, great business and political success, but it keeps silent about whether those people, those great accomplishers where happy or not. Many were not happy at all. As a matter of fact the wealthier person is the more desperate he is, because having it all, he is still not satisfied, not fulfilled and he suspects he never will. Not one great accomplisher was happy, with exception of those who chose Freedom. You may read exciting stories about the accomplishers, of their great success, but all these stories are fiction and have only crumbs of truth in them and those pity crumbs are not really truthful, because one who wrote the story is not a man of Freedom. He could not prevent his ego from getting involved and ego always distorts truth.

Nevertheless, we believe these stories and dream to become accomplishers like our heroes: winners in fleeting accomplishments and losers in life.

"Those who don't know **history** are destined to repeat it." Says British Statesman Edmund Burke. Since the 17th century this saying survived and is repeated in books and encyclopedias. But this statement is utterly ridiculous for two reasons. The first reason is that no one knows true history. Another reason is: there could not be two situations that are totally the same, especially when they are separated in time, that's because there are no two persons that can be exactly the same. The second reason is obvious, but why is it that no one can ever know a true history? Here is example.

British historian, whose name was also Edmund, spent over 40 years writing *History of the World.* When this monumental job was nearly completed, he destroyed his work, burned it in his fireplace.

It so happened that a man was killed just outside of Edmund's home in front of several witnesses and the killer ran away. When Burke came to the scene, he asked each witness about what happened and he received four different stories. He couldn't believe it: a murder happened just before their eyes, and each person saw it differently, each one had his own story. Burk came back home and burned his entire work. If witnesses cannot agree on something they just saw, he said, what could I say about Buddha or Christ, about Julius Cesar or Alexander the Great?

This is why there can be no known truth about history, especially when every leader wants his country to have a respectful history. The history of Russia was rewritten four times during soviet regime. In the U.S. children are still taught that it was United States that won WWII, and say little about Russia that actually won the war. And this war happened less than seven decades ago.

Thus, there cannot be a true historical account of anything, anyone, or of any accomplishment. However, it is a fact that no great or small accomplisher was truly happy with life. The explanation is simple: it is not material success that makes one truly happy in life, but growth in Love and Awareness. If one grows in Love and Awareness, he will simultaneously become more successful, and he will live a life of happiness, but if he neglects Love and Awareness, he experiences only a glimpse of happiness and much sorrow, regardless of how successful he becomes. It happens this way because only accomplishment in inner growth can make one truly happy, all other accomplishments are only icing on the cake of true happiness.

If we are not successful, some program within us is sabotaging our goals. To identify the program, we need to set goals and keep releasing on them until we either achieve them or decide we are no longer interested in pursuing them. In the process we learn what impairs our success and releases the blocks.

We are given a choice to conceive a thought, idea, to act, or to not. Every emotion is abstraction, every doubt is impediment, every thought is limitation. Negative thoughts and emotions, especially those hidden in subconscious, are grouping into major blockages toward success in any area of life.

When we mold our goal with the flame of Awareness, it is bound to materialize. Nothing else is necessary. When a goal is decisively conceived, envisioned, released upon, and let to be, it is accomplished in the mind of the beholder and you calmly continue to do whatever is needed to be done.

Some people are born with this inner conviction. When they set a goal, in their mind it is already accomplished and so it gets accomplished. Everyone else needs to learn how to do it with releasing.

Instead of the brakes of WANTING, apply an attitude of calm conviction. You're convinced you already HAVE what you *allowed* yourself to have. Every success story has this in common: a calm conviction, a confidence of accomplishment before the goal was actually accomplished.

As you continue working on your goal with such a conviction, the necessary elements will fall into place. You sow the seed of the goal in your mind with conviction and confidence. The process is similar to sowing seeds of grain in the ground. Like the seed in the ground, the seed of your goal must not be disturbed with doubts and concerns. It needs to be left alone to germinate, and sprout.

Not everything we're trying to accomplish may be good for us in the long run. Neither Abraham Lincoln nor John F. Kennedy knew this, along with countless others.

Ideally, all emotions associated with the goal, both negative and positive, need to be released. Your goal will then be accomplished if it is beneficial for you in the long run. It will not be accomplished if it might hurt you in the future. This way, you will create in your life only what is beneficial.

It is your essence—awareness that through intuitive channel provides you with necessary information, and is behind your every accomplishment. You may hear and follow its advice, or silence it with your mental buzz. Usually, the latter is the case. However, when you're released of all mental influence, both positive and negative, you will heed the advice.

When something is accomplished, it is usually left to live its own life and is helped only when help is necessary. There is no need for constant emotional involvement. There may be the need for much 'help' in the course of a project's life, but the project is already accomplished and it is finished as far as its creator is concerned. Why worry about something that already has been done? But usually this is not the case. It may be difficult to believe in something you don't see. "How can this releasing help?" You ask, "And how can it raise the money needed for the project? It is philosophy; what I need is cash." And you keep going, pushing on the accelerator and slamming on the brakes at the same time.

Make a chart for every goal:

1. On one side of the chart describe the goal in pencil to allow for revisions. When formulating your goal, never use the word WANT. Instead, write word ALLOW: "I allow myself to experience a wonderful relationship now." "I ALLOW myself to buy a new car now." Every

goal must be written and thought of in present tense. If you set it in the future, it may remain in the future.

2. Release on the goal as follows: read the goal, then ask, "What comes to mind when I read this?" Record the feeling or thought and release it. Repeat this step as necessary.

3. When you feel released and positive (when you are in CAP: Courageousness, Acceptance or, Peace) and loving your goal, turn the chart over and list the action you can take to achieve the goal. Release your feelings related to each action. If an action step occurs to you at any point as you're releasing on the goal in step 2, turn the page over and note it (in this step 3).

4. Review and add to your charts periodically for more releasing.

5. Repeat the process until you achieve the goal or decide that you don't need it.

If not destined to be successful, your ability to become more aware and loving is always with you and can help you to turn the tables on your destiny. Play your game of desires and goals with ever increasing awareness, but remember that road of desire leads nowhere, only Freedom brings true satisfaction.

> The worldly hope men set their hearts upon
> Turns ashes—or it prospers; and anon,
> Like snow upon the desert's dusty face
> Lighting a little hour or two—is gone.

Most people seek money as completion of all their aspirations. Some people seek a truly good life. But rarely are they interested in the ultimate. When they get to the place where life becomes nice and easy and comfortable, they stop caring about their growth.

Some people might get quite far, says Lester. The couples get along exceptionally well. Life is a ball—and then they level off. Several years later, they feel awful. Business is not as good as it used to be. They get headaches and they're frustrated. They really are miserable. So there they get stuck. They can't remain happy, because they will never be satisfied until they go all the way.

When you are ready, do this experiment: set aside a day for releasing. Do not write or read, don't make notes... do releasing only. Release every emotion, let go of every thought that comes to your mind... and something wonderful may happen.

Just sit relax and release... and awareness will down, it will flood you from within. It will pour from your own spring. Just sit in silence. When thoughts come—watch and let them pass.

***

Anything impossible, no matter how impossible becomes possible when we are completely released on it.

The following is an example of how Lester was accomplishing his goals after he went free. While reading this, pay attention to the spontaneity of irrevocable Decision and the lack of effort.

In 1953, Lester began buying apartment buildings with no cash down. He would either run them for profit or sell them for quick profit. Within six months, he had acquired well over a million dollars equity in property.

"I started in the real estate business with no cash and bought apartment houses using mortgages and loans. With no effort, I acquired twenty-three apartment houses with twenty to forty units each. I found it was easy to do.

"Every deal had to be a very harmonious one. Everyone in it had to gain. If there was a broker involved, I made sure he got his full commission. The seller benefited by getting what he wanted, his building sold. And if there was a lawyer involved, he got his share. Everyone benefited in every deal. That's the way all deals should be. There's no need for anyone to suffer. Everyone should get what he wants out of it. Everyone should benefit.

"Every seller wants to sell. Every buyer wants, to buy. I found that harmony is the basic law of the universe, when we're in tune with it, things can be done with little effort."

"What's the next step?" he wondered. He had proven he could apply his new theory to business, he had over a million dollars; what was left to prove?

Then it occurred to him that the need to accumulate wealth was not security. It could all be lost. Also, the need for accumulation indicated a lack of conviction in one's ability to produce what one needed at will. Therefore, he decided, "From here on, I have everything I need as I need it," and proceeded to test out still another theory.

"It was a few days before Christmas, cold, and I wanted a short vacation of two weeks in warm country.

Los Angeles was far away from New York City so I said, "Well, I'm having a vacation in Los Angeles over the Christmas New Year holidays."

"With full confidence that "everything is A-okay and taken care of," I packed a bag and walked out of the house. Within a block, I bumped into a man I hadn't seen for many, many years who said, "Hey, Lester! I've been looking for you. Remember that money I owed you? I've wanted to pay you. I didn't know what happened to you."

And he handed me enough cash to buy a round-trip ticket to Los Angeles, which I did, and immediately left.

"When I got to Los Angeles, it occurred to me to call an old friend who said, "Oh, I'm so happy you called, Lester, we just got a new apartment, we have an extra room and you must stay with us. Where are you?" And they picked me up.

The next morning I was in the kitchen thinking, "Well, gee, here I am in Los Angeles without a car. It's impossible to get around without one." And I said, "Well, that's taken care of," and I dropped it.

"Next thought came, "Call Burl." He was an old friend I had driven with from New York to Los Angeles some years earlier. I called Burl, and he said, "I've been thinking of you, Lester. Where are you? I want to see you and I'm coming right over." And he was there in a matter of about fifteen minutes.

And we're having coffee over the kitchen table and without my asking, he puts his hand in his pocket, takes his car keys out, slides them across the table to me and says "You've got my car as long as you stay here. I have no need for it. I'm living near the studio and I walk to work." I thanked him. Now I had everything I needed.

"After about ten days, I got the feeling that I wanted to go back to New York. It was about January 3rd. I called TWA and they said, "Oh, I'm sorry. We have no reservations for thirty days, all taken up. And we can't even put you on the waiting list because the waiting lists each have thirty or more people."

I just said "Thank you," hung up and said to myself, "Well, who needs a reservation? When I feel like going, I'll go!" So, the next morning, I woke up and asked myself, "Do I want to go?" And I said, "Yeah, I think I want to go."

I packed my bags and got down to the airport about ten o'clock, asked where the planes depart for New York, went to the gate, and a man was loading a plane for New York. I said, "Are there any no-shows?" He said, "Yes, there is one. But wait until I load everyone. Just stand here."

"While he was loading, a woman asked the same question. He said, "I don't know, madam, but if you'll stand behind this man, we'll find out." And he put her behind me.

He loaded the plane, walked right toward me, reached around me, took this woman by the arm and put her on the plane.

As far as I was concerned, everything was 100% okay![14]

He came back to me and his jaw dropped! His mouth fell open when he realized what he had done. So I had to calm him down, instead of him calming me down. And after I calmed him down, I said, "Well, when's your next plane?"

He said, "In about an hour. Oh, there it is coming in right now."

"Well, he put me on that plane, which got me to New York two hours earlier than the other one. It was a non-stop flight, the first one I ever had cross-country. At that time, they usually made at least one stop. Non-stop flights were new and few. This was in the days of the DC-6s and the Constellations; there were no jets at that time. It wasn't easy for them to make cross-country non-stop flights.

"Then I remembered that when I'd hung up and said, "Who needs a reservation?" I said, "Not only that, I'll have my first non-stop flight cross-country." And that was

---

[14] This kind of unshakable confidence makes all the difference between success and failure (y.s.).

the reason for his putting me off the first flight and putting me on the next one.

"And so I got back to New York-started out with no money, I came back with no money."

Later, a trip around the world again proved the same principle of abundance: "I have everything I need as I need it."

After Lester's tremendous breakthrough into peace in 1952, that awareness of the truth never left him. Whether he was doing a real estate deal, or visiting his family, or sharing his experience with others, he was always aware of and residing in his own inner Beingness of peace. People loved being with him because he saw them in the same way that he saw himself: all-beautiful, all knowing, all-powerful, all-perfect, peaceful. This powerful perception projected itself to each receptive person and activated that inner core in which each was all those things. Many people had experiences of this truth of themselves while in his presence, and they were eager to have more and to hear of his experiences.

Religion and Freedom

"How sweet is mortal sovereignty!" – think some;
Others – "How blessed the paradise to come!"
Ah, take the cash in hand and wave the rest;
Oh, the brave music of a distant drum!

Mortal sovereignty here means material success. Paradise to come: uncertain hope for paradise after death. Cash in hand: wealth of Awareness, Love and Freedom that brings happiness with no sorrow. Brave music: determination and confidence in your own abilities. Distant drum: unshakable faith in success.

The god of the cannibals will be a cannibal, of the crusaders a crusader, and of the merchants a merchant.

Ralph Waldo Emerson

There is no god that punishes. But there is god that rewards: a god of Love. We, birds of Love, are born to fly free and to reward with Love all creation.

Historically and today, every faith has people of high Awareness, who bring Love to the others.

Awareness and Love 'created' people like Buddha, Jesus, Yogananda, the Prophet, Bodhidharma, Huang Po, Lao Tzu, hundreds of thousands if not millions free human beings. Needless to say these people—the very best of humanity—became what they were because they realized themselves being boundless ocean of Awareness, Love. There are as many ways to Freedom as there are people, and each way is as unique as each person's life. But in the end, only realization of being Awareness and Love could set us free.

Awareness and Love are at the core of every religion, and for many seekers of the past, religion often played role of a stepping stone to Freedom. It is practically impossible to become free while sitting in the church or mosque, listening to sermons; no one ever found Freedom in the crowd. Those who craved Freedom were leaving the world, taking with them only idea of God that would become Awareness and Love. Living in deserts and forests, far from the world, they realized that life knows no negativity, so they cleansed themselves of their own negativity and of that one of the world; they opened within an infinite ocean of Love and became highly aware. They started as religious people, and they became free people, free of all dogmas and concepts, of attachments and aversions, they accepted and loved all people, the entire universe, they became Love.

It is all right to be religious, to believe in God, Allah or Krishna. It is all right to believe in anything. There were many who believed in planets and went free. The secret is not in the object of belief, but in belief itself; secret lies with faith. It is faith that moves mountains. Whatever is the subject of faith, our faith must be unshakable, it must be limitless, and what is limitless faith if not true Love. When faith is limited, it is partial, it is fragmented, it is not Love that knows no limits.

A man went through six years of the war in the infantry. He couldn't even remember how many companies he had served in, all destroyed to the last man, but he didn't get a scar. He faced death so many times, that it became his companion, and he never feared it. He had a pendant given to him by his grandmother, who said it would keep him safe in the war, and he believed without a shadow of doubt that it would keep him safe as long as he was wearing it. He believed it would save him in the war, but when the war ended...

He had great faith in this pendant, which entirely banished his fear of death while he was at war. He was fearless there, but he dreaded heights, and paid no attention to this fear. He never stepped out to the balcony, but he ended his life jumping from a high-rise. Instead of releasing fear of heights, he kept either dwelling on it or run away from it. He didn't know how to release, he didn't know that he could have extend his faith in the pendant to the time of peace, but if he did, he could have died peacefully. This man was the father of my friend and I knew him well. If his incredible faith in his pendant would have been all-encompassing it would also take him beyond his fear of heights, but he limited his faith to the time of war, because his grandmother said it would protect him at war.

Those who found their Freedom had no limits to their faith, to their Love. Those who didn't dissolve all limits are not free.

Following in steps of those who reached Freedom, we accept the entire universe, all religions and all people. "But organized religion is wrong," wrote to me one reader, "it makes people slaves, takes money from the poor and is getting ever wealthier. It separates and divides; it supports wars and genocides... how it is possible to accept all that?" My answer was in one sentence: Love is the answer.

When there is only Love within, it doesn't exclude something by not accepting it or in any other way. Love knows no exceptions. When there is only Love, we are one with the universe. The universe and everything in it is part of ourselves, it is within us. To cut off anything in the universe would be the same as to cut off our own arm when it is ailing.

Christianity teaches to have faith in God, Islam—in Allah, Hindus suggest to put faith in Krishna, Divine Mother, Zen implies faith in yourself, Sufis have faith in Love of God... Every religion emphasizes utmost importance of faith. Saints of every religion reached Freedom with help of the unshakable faith. How is it possible to acquire this kind of faith? It becomes possible with Love. Love is tangible, it is something we do. But we need to open to total Love within. Being Love and

111

have an unshakable faith in perfection makes us perfect. But even little negativity, one little doubt will destroy it all.

This is why as we expand our Love, we banish all negativity, throw away judgments, let go of resistance and release all fears. Love knows only Oneness and Harmony of all existence. As we see the world, so are we. When we see it as one harmonious, beautiful place, we are loving and peaceful, because we could see the world as such only when we are nothing but Love. At this eternal moment we are Awareness *that is aware of itself*: we are aware of ourselves, of our oneness and harmony, and as we rise even higher in Awareness, we realize that we are Love and Awareness that is forever aware of itself in every detail of creation.

My friend is a doctor, he believes that after death he will go to a better place called Paradise or Heaven, because he strives to be a good person and helps others. Many believe the same idea. Any belief is OK for the believer, but this kind of belief unlikely leads to a total Love and Freedom. Total Love is selfless, it doesn't do anything for an exchange like when I am good, I will end up in Paradise. Total Love has no exclusion, it does not discriminate between so called good and bad people of all faiths, it loves everyone unconditionally.

When we allow our mind to project our life into the future, we become blind to the present. To a blind person, all around him is a horrible world of darkness, greed, crime, suffering and sorrow, with no happiness. As soon as we awaken, the same world turns into a world of beauty, harmony and oneness, marvelous world of Love and happiness. Whether one is religious or not, why to wait until death? Who knows what is behind this curtain of the unknown? Why not live a happy life today? Why not awaken to Paradise now, for this Earth is Paradise indeed. All one needs to do is to wake up and recognize its beauty, harmony and oneness within and without. It is good to remember that life happens only now, this moment that Paradise is always here, where we are at the moment, for life is only this instant, which with higher awareness becomes eternity. Yesterday is gone and thinking of Paradise in tomorrow will always be pushing it further into the future that never comes.

Though every concept is a limitation, while on the road to happiness, we utilize some useful concepts. Eventually we need to discard even a concept of releasing but to become releasing, which means to become capable of releasing thought or emotion at the time of origination, and to be an impartial witness. We need eventually to discard the concept of oneness in order to become one with all creation, which means, be ready to accept any part of creation, including all people with their egos, concepts ideas and acts. Undoubtedly, concept of Love will also need to be released so we become Love, as well as the concept of Awareness needs to be let go of in order for us to become Awareness.

It is useful to watch our own reaction when we are presented with an idea disagreeable to us. If we become defensive, irritated, upset... if such a presentation provokes any emotion – we are bound and have a long way to go, because we are at the very beginning of the road and demonstrate low awareness. Freedom begins with acceptance, which is Love. Not only Freedom, it is a common sense to accept another the way he is.

The eternal question remains: is Awareness also a creator or is it only a provider, and sustainer of creation? Those who are free know the answer, but when sages are trying to relate it to us, much confusion arises. In the beginning it is hard to accept that we are the creators. Indeed, if 200 years ago we believed the religious assertion that human history was only 6,000 years old, today some believe it is over 300 million years young and humanity could have existed in previous cycles of our universe. Awareness is beyond action, thus it is beyond creation. It is possible that our universe exists cyclically forever. Only man is capable of creating.

There are two 'religions', Tao and Zen that do not use concept of God the Creator. They teach awareness, responsibility, acceptance and letting go.

Zen is an abbreviation of the Japanese words Zenno and Zenna, derived from the Chinese word Ch'an (meditation), which in turn was derived from the Sanskrit word dhyana.

Zen is described by Christmas Humphries, Founder of the Buddhist Society in London, as "the apotheosis of Buddhism," and a "direct assault upon the citadel of Truth, without reliance upon concepts or the use of scripture, ritual or vow." It doesn't deny scriptures, but none of them is considered to be authority.

In China, Zen is also called *hsin tsung*, which means "the teaching of the Mind," referring of course to the Buddha-Mind and Enlightenment. It is also the understanding and perfecting of the mind, for in the perfecting of the mind there is the discovery of the Freedom. This is a central purpose of Zen. The term Pure Mind is used as the equivalent of Awareness and thus Zen becomes the pursuit of Awareness. The essential means of Zen are meditation, inspiration and none-artificiality.

In his introduction to a four volume set entitled *The Taoist Classics* Thomas Cleary provides the following description of Tao:

"...It may mean a path, a way, a principle, a method, a doctrine, a system of order; and it also may mean the matrix, structure, and reality of the universe itself. Every art and science is called a tao, or a way; but the source of everything, the fountain of all art and science, is called the Tao, or the Way.

114

Taoism is based, first and foremost, on the experience of this universal Way, the essential reality through which all derivative ways might be comprehended.

Considering the ultimate nature of the Way to be inherently beyond the bounds of human conception, ancient Taoists sought traces of the Way in the patterns of events taking place in the natural world, the social world, and the inner world of the individual psyche. Eventually the scope of the Way led them to undertake the investigation of vast domains of knowledge and experience.

While followers of Taoism thus branched out into many different fields of research and work, those interested primarily in the essential Tao continued to focus on perfecting the mastery of human nature and life in three critical areas: individual well-being, social harmony, and accelerated evolution within consciousness. These three bases were believed to form the foundation of overall human development, the guiding lights of the arts and sciences.

Through generations of applying the Tao to these three basic domains of life, extraordinary accomplishments in the maintenance of physical vitality, fostering of sensitive and effective relations between people, and development of latent mental powers, including spontaneous insight and foreknowledge, came to be recognized as byproducts of working with the Way.

Furthermore, according to the ethos of the Way, these developments, once realized, were not to be guarded possessively but put to the service of humanity. In accordance with the elusive nature of the Way, the beneficial results of its application by individuals were not to be paraded proudly before others but to be diffused in an inconspicuous yet effective manner."

Thomas Cleary holds a Ph.D. in Eastern Asian Languages and Civilizations from Harvard University. He is the translator of over fifty volumes of Buddhist,

Taoist, Confucian and Islamic texts from Sanskrit, Chinese, Japanese, and Arabic – including the best selling *Art of War.*

Meditation

Growing in Awareness[15] is inseparable from releasing of conceptual thinking and negative emotional content. When one is strong enough, he may rise beyond influence of conceptual thinking and emotional content. This usually happens after we have quite freed ourselves from considerable part of the subconscious baggage.

When our experience, no matter how grand it is, can be interpreted by our conscious mind, the experience will always fall short from "experiencing" reality of Awareness, for it is inexplicable. Reality of Awareness is our innermost natural state of being, it is our Beingness, as Lester called it, not an experience that can be interpreted. Awareness cannot be interpreted and does not need any interpretation, for it is beyond the conceptual mind with its interpreting.

> You know, my friends, how long since in my house
> For new marriage I did make carouse:
> Divorced old barren reason from my bed,
> And took the daughter of the vine to spouse.

Barren reason: dogmatic knowledge. The daughter of the vine: meditation.

---

[15] We do not really 'grow in Awareness', but free ourselves from the influence of thinking process and subconscious' data: free ourselves from limitations.

Meditation is awareness of Awareness and becoming 'It' – supremely aware, which is Freedom. This is a true meaning of meditation. It is also an understanding of what life is in its wholeness, when life is no longer fragmented by the mind, when it is no longer divided into 'good' and 'bad'. Repetitions of certain mantra, chanting or concentration are not meditation. These techniques will temporarily calm the mind and help prepare it for the meditation.

The first step in meditation (and last) is to learn witnessing the mind's movement, no matter where it goes. Only then will meditation come, when we are being imperturbable and serene in watching our thoughts and emotions finally disappear.

Silence reached with the help of thought is not useful. Silence that is reached through realizing the source of the thought is very helpful. When thought becomes aware of its source, when it realizes that it is never free and is always old, then will silence come.

For example, when we are fully aware of watching a play or a movie without either judging it or forgetting ourselves—this also is meditation. Meditation is a state of whole or Pure Mind not contaminated by thought or emotion. Meditation does not have a particular technique or an authority. It is probably the most beautiful of life's arts. Impartial witnessing of ourselves and life with everything in it, is also meditation that may be practiced anywhere, anytime.

The mind uncontrolled and unguided will drag us down, down forever. It will render us, kill us; while the mind controlled and guided will save us, free us, said Vivekananda, the first spiritual ambassador to the US from India and foremost mediator. Meditation is not a physical culture; it is peacefulness itself. It is the actualization of wisdom that comes extended to our everyday life.

When I have started "meditating", I could not sit quietly even a few minutes. Everything was calling to my attention, provoking thoughts and action. All else would suddenly become very important. This false sense of importance was created by the mind. Make a decision to meditate and begin with a session of five minutes long. It is helpful to take a brisk 10 - 15 minutes walk before meditation or to do a simple physical or breathing exercise.

Find a spot where you will not be disturbed. Ventilate the room and keep it cool. Place a small cushion on top of the seat of the chair and a woolen rug on top of the cushion. Lower part of the rug should be long enough for your feet to be placed over it. The wool is used to prevent the energy from escaping. Cover your shoulders with woolen sweater when cold. Sit on a cushion in a manner as comfortable as possible, wear loose clothing.

Relax...

Keep your spine straight without straining, your chin —parallel to the floor. Hold your body straight without leaning to the left or the right, forward or backward. Your ears should be in alignment with your shoulders, and your nose in a straight line with your navel. Keep the tongue at the roof of the mouth and close your lips. Eyes are closed or slightly open and breathing is quiet through the nostrils.

Place your hands on top of thighs with palms facing up, small fingers touching the lower abdomen. Get use to the pose of sitting comfortably. Do not touch the back of the chair with your back. Do not put any support between your back and the back of the chair. From the very start learn to sit straight without any support. I am a very ordinary person and I learned how to meditate with a group for 2 to 4 hours without intermission. I noticed that most of the people who use something to support their back, get up every 45 minutes, etc. But you can learn to do it right and without intermission, from the very start. Just make a decision to do it right and do it. There is nothing difficult to it. It is the mind that is trying all sorts of excuses.

Before you begin meditating take several slow, deep breaths. Hold your body erect, allowing your breathing to become normal again. Do not follow your breath, do not fix your thoughts on forms or colors, do not fix your thoughts on space, God, angels or devils, or four basic elements (fire, water, etc.). Do not fix your thoughts on what you ever saw, heard or memorized. All imaginations and recollections should be excluded from your mind, even an idea of exclusion should be excluded.

Do not strain. Do not ask questions. Questions cannot be answered for you; answers will come from within. Just follow the procedure. The mind loves questioning. Do not let it find any excuse to distract you. Time will come and there will be answer to your every question. Most of your questions will simply drop away as unimportant.

In meditation force nothing. Be persistent, very patient and intense. Learn to let meditation happen to you; do not try to make anything happen... Always persevere in using a little extra effort to meditate a little longer, be a little extra patient. That's the only effort you should use. And remember, all that you are learning is how to peacefully watch your mind, how to be a witness.

Feel your spine and, from time to time, very subtly straighten it, 'pool' it up without strain. It must be a very gentle feeling, like a feather flying...

The first step and the last are to learn watching the mind. If in the beginning we will learn the witnessing of our conscious mind, which is the easily accessible part of the Belief system, in the end of this process we may come

to witnessing the deeper recesses of our Believe system –
the subconscious, which contains information we brought
to this life from the realm of Awareness, as well as
records of our gene system.

We know that we think, but we don't know how
thoughts happen. We identify with the content of the
mind and allow ourselves to be disturbed by it. Through
quiet watching we learn to witness these disturbances
without them affecting us. Eventually, this process will
help to eliminate problems. Not that the problems will stop
from arising.... Living in the body cannot be without
problems, but they will not affect our state of calm any longer.
Being at peace, we will be able to allow the right solution to
come in sooner. When emotions and thoughts arise during
meditation, it is helpful to remember that everything we have
in our mind was put there, or allowed to be put there by
ourselves. It is the influence of the hidden subconscious
content that handicaps us most.

Watch your mind. Many thoughts will crowd there;
watch them sailing infinitely through your mind. In the
beginning trains of thoughts will consistently run through
your mind. This train consists of symbols, ideas,
tendencies, emotions and concepts. We don't identify
with its content, or feel that it is part of us; we know it is
not of our reality. There is something in us, an identity,
which is distinct and separate from this mental content.
When in deeper meditation our senses are shut, we have
even greater sense of identity, a sense of Self, which is
Awareness. We learn to witness the train, because it is not
us, but a product of our making.

Anything that is in our mind belongs to that mental
train. We need only to observe it, even when in the
beginning it is not clear where the train comes from and
where it goes. We learn to never suppress or struggle
with our thoughts and, never argue with anything on that

our train. We witness and let it all pass without identifying with it. If the train continues to linger and dominate the mind, we simply watch it for as long as necessary, as if we are sitting in the car at the intersection, waiting for some train to rumble by…. Eventually, it has to pass and disappear. When a stray thought crosses a blue nothingness of our Mind, we will simply see it go.

We will find that each day the mind's antics are becoming less violent and it is becoming calmer. We will also learn to be aware of what we are experiencing. Aware of each experience fully, as it takes place in our every day life, we will not try to run away or hide from the unavoidable 'bad' experiences.

Whatever our experience in meditation, we will not get attached to it and will not prolong or repeat it. We will treat every experience as we treat a thought: be aware of it coming and going. When one is truly free, there are no thoughts in meditation and no experiences. Awareness will 'experience' only itself and the difference between meditation and life will disappear.

During the first several minutes of meditation, if it is too difficult to just watch thoughts and emotions, we may use the following techniques:
- become aware of the spot between the eyebrows, or
- employ a single thought, like "What am I", or
- watch your breath.

This will not be meditation, but the techniques may be helpful in the very beginning, providing that we use it for just a few minutes. In each case do it intensely. At the same time watch your body for any slight movement: the body must be absolutely still. I found that at the start, by taking attention from the body with the mind intensely involved in one of the above techniques helps to still the body sooner. As soon as body is still, I drop the introductory assistance and begin watching the mind. It is also possible to discover some means of your own that will help you to still the body.

During meditation we may expand our ability at becoming Awareness. With every exhalation enlarge your presence beyond the body, then beyond room, house, street, include the town, a country, the globe, material universe and the worlds beyond...

Truth is perfect and complete. It is present in the process of watching thoughts, as well as in our every experience. Buddha was meditating six years, Bodhidharma – nine. However, we must remember that we may speed up nothing. Buddha and Bodhidharma did not happen over night. So be diligent and patient for as it was said by Ecclesiastes, to everything there is a season and a time to every purpose under the heaven. This saying hides a profound meaning within. Just look at your past carefully and you surely will notice that whenever you were impatient, pushing, whenever you acted driven by emotions and not in accord with your intuition, you created problems. Meditation helps to learn that every effortless experience is an expression of truth, but longing and striving is of no avail.

We must be genuinely interested in heightening our ability to become Awareness, even if in the beginning it serves our material goals. Unless we feel genuine curiosity and attraction to meditation, it will be wrong to force ourselves just for the sake of it or because someone said it is good thing to do. There is a big difference between forcing and disciplining oneself. Discipline is necessary for any practice, while forcing is always wrong. And there is fine line between disciplining and forcing... just watch carefully that you are not stepping over it.

The practice of witnessing is an attempt to realize what we are. Because Freedom is not an experience, witnessing and meditation are not Freedom but they provide us with glimpses of Freedom and can certainly lead us to Freedom.

Our search among books may lead to the depths of material knowledge, but it is not the way to know oneself. "For in much [human] wisdom is much grief: and he who increases knowledge increases sorrow," says Ecclesiastes, meaning material knowledge.

At some point in our practice we may experience fear, apathy, grief and other negative emotions. This happens because with the conscious mind calmed, we enter our subconscious—an iceberg, made of everything we have ever experienced. Once we have entered this realm, we may as well become a witness to it. It is the most effective method of releasing, because being an illusion, thoughts and emotions of the past disintegrate as they are being calmly watched.

There are several reasons why you may find group meditation helpful, especially in the beginning. Group disciplines, encourages and creates collective energy that positively affects everyone in the group.

One who is free, will fully experience life with its array of emotions and thoughts, and will never become affected or attached to any of them. Beyond any concept, Freedom is us being Awareness, our true nature, a mystery. Then we also understand the meaning of Acceptance, true Love, Oneness, Harmony.

Practicing meditation in the morning or evening, or at any leisure time during the day, we will soon realize our mental burdens dropping away, and that we are gaining access to intuitive power previously unnoticed. Meditation will incomparably improve the quality of our life, greatly contributing to our happiness and success. There are many who have practiced meditation and obtained its fruits. Do not doubt its possibilities because of the simplicity of the method. The Truth can only be found within. Every experience is a door to Freedom and Truth, but meditation is a wide open door.

We know nothing and in truth, and will never learn anything. We may only experience a suitable state of being very close to the center, being close to becoming Awareness. It is only when we find ourselves beyond mind, we will be approaching the reality of light and greater inspiration. We will begin to probe into the world of ideas and realize we are entering an unknown realm of Awareness—the source of life.

The final goal of meditation is Samadhi, the state of tranquility. It may also be called a state of sleepless sleep, glimpses of which we may experience while falling asleep or immediately upon awakening. It is somewhat similar but not the same state that we reach while having an out-of-body experience.

When we are more aware, every experience in our life becomes meditation with the real us being in charge. It is simple, but not easily learned, because "fully aware" means to be spontaneously in control, which also means not wanting to control or change anything but accepting and loving all. Not wanting control of anything also means complete absence of resistance to anything what-so-ever. This is Enlightenment—a priceless fruit of moment-to-moment meditation, called life.

Steps to Happiness and Freedom

We must want Freedom more than we want approval, control and security.

Decide you can do the Method and be imperturbable.

See all your feelings culminate in three wants: the want of approval, control and security/survival. See it immediately and immediately let go of the want of approval, want to control and the want of security/survival.

Make releasing constant.

If you are stuck, let go of wanting to control your stuckness.

Each time you release you are happier and lighter. If you release continually, you will be continually happier and lighter.

Get everything only by releasing.

Practice witnessing while releasing.

Take responsibility for everything in your life.

Take all your joy from within.

Be loving and all giving.

Be yourself.

An outright importance of Love is discussed in more detail in the *Autobiography* that follows.

Lester Levenson
Autobiography

Alas, the spring should vanish with the rose!
That Youth's sweet-scented manuscript should close!
The nightingale that in the branches sang,
Ah, whence and whither flown again, who knows!

To everything there is a season, and a time to every purpose under Heaven. Sweet promise of happiness has gone... It is time to open Love within, to love each present moment completely, to let the future take care of itself and fully enjoy the wonder and beauty of each instant.

A letter from Lester

Greetings,

Almost forty years ago, with my back to the wall and only three months to live, I was forced to search for the answers to life. I decided to ask myself what we all want, and the answer came to me: we all want to be happy!

I had spent my entire life looking for happiness and security in making money, having personal relationships and keeping busy. But I only achicvcd happiness for a short period of time. Somehow happiness still eluded me.

I wondered how could I get all the things I want and be happy all the time, too.

Most of the great philosophers have told us that our basic inherent nature is happiness. So what is it that happens that causes us to lose what is already ours? The answer is: Our feelings cover up happiness and keep it hidden from us.

The key to secure the happiness that is yours… forever… is to discover how to discharge the negative feelings you've accumulated. By discharging these negative feelings, you will not only increase the happiness in your life, but everything else will get better too! Money, health, relationships, looks, you name it!

It is so simple and it's the answer you've been looking for.

Love, Lester

Introduction

When I think this book is going to be about me, I get cringing feelings. It's not easy for me to be an ego and yet I must talk as an ego in order to communicate.

Once you see your real inner Self, it's very difficult to identify yourself as a separate individual, an ego.

But I can go through with telling of story.

I fell into something that everyone is looking for. I had no idea it was there. All my desires were fulfilled; all my miseries dropped away; all my sickness disappeared.

I came into an exalted state of happiness, so tremendous it is difficult to describe.

Joy is what everyone in the world is seeking, very few people are finding.

The way this fell upon me can be given to others, so that it can fall upon them also.

I'm talking about something that hardly anyone has yet experienced. How can I describe it?

There are no limitations on anything in any direction. There is the ability to do anything by the mere thought of it. Yet it is more than that.

Imagine the highest joy you can have, multiply it by a hundred and tell me what it is.

You will only feel it to the degree you're capable off feeling it. It can't be gotten intellectually.

Imagine being madly in love with your mate and embracing your mate, with your mind on nothing else but the joy of the embrace. Now double that for two people, quadruple it for four people, and then make it a billion times greater by including the four billion people on earth.

That's the feeling.

Life Before Consciousness (B.C.)

LOVE IS TRUST

I was an average guy seeking happiness in money and women, battling my way through life like everyone else. Never finding it, I continued banging my head so hard on the brick wall of the world that I almost smashed my brains out. I had ulcers, migraine, jaundice, kidney stones and finally a coronary attack which brought me near death.

That extremity drove me into the right direction, to the knowledge of what life is all about.

This knowledge gave me contentment, a peace, which cannot be disturbed.

People can yell at me, scream, do anything, and the peace in the background never changes.

It's there all the time.

I was a rebel against society and I banged my head on its brick wall until I discovered the way out.

Now that I have discovered it, others don't have to bang their head so hard to find it. It's available for anyone who wants it.

Anyone who really wants knowledge and Freedom gets it. All you need is <u>you</u> – and the desire for it. <u>You</u> are the book. <u>You</u> are the real book. An intense desire for it opens up the real you to you.

That's what happens. But we're so plagued with blindness today that we need a teacher, who knows and can keep pointing out the way.

Within you is unlimited power, knowledge and intelligence. You just open yourself up to that which you subconsciously already know, have always known and always will know.

From the beginning I was bewildered. I could not understand the world. I rebelled against it, yet I wanted to do right, be right with the world. From post-college days on until 1952, I just kept trying to do what I thought was the correct thing.

I had a degree in physics and I wanted to be the world's greatest physicist. I was graduated from college in 1931. There were no jobs for physicists then, so I shifted to engineering. I worked as an aeronautical, civil, mechanical, electrical, marine and construction engineer.

I'd get a job and wouldn't last a year because it just didn't feel right. So I'd go into another type of engineering and yet another. I tried going into business for myself. I'd get successful, lose interest, and then lose the business.

I just kept changing, never understanding why until 1952. Then I realized what I was looking for was not in a job or business. No job, no business, even when I was into it and was successful, could give it to me.

During my whole life, I was unconsciously seeking what I discovered in 1952.

I was born in Elizabeth, New Jersey, on July 19, 1909.

My earliest recollection was of water. I always loved the water.

When I was four I used to walk two long blocks and two short blocks to a large docking and recreation wharf in Elizabeth port.

I'd climb up on a wall at the edge of the dock – it was about two feet high and about three feet wide - and I'd just lie down on it with my head over the edge watching the water flow by for hours at a time, for so many hours that my mother went looking for me, when she found me, she almost collapsed - seeing me, a tot, hanging over the edge of the dock. She gently took me by the hand and with a smile said, "Come on home." She never scolded me. She just told me I shouldn't do that because I might fall in.

But I never fell in. I didn't believe it. Liking the water so much, I'd wander back to the dock. Even as a child, I wasn't believing what others told me. My mother warned me that green bananas made people sick. I used to love bananas. I had eaten green bananas and had not gotten sick. So to prove my point, one day I ate a dozen green bananas and said, "Look, Ma! I feel fine!" She just laughed.

My mother used to get delight from me. Here I was, so little and acting like a grown-up, teaching her by proving things to her.

My mother was an unusually loving person. Never in her whole lifetime did she ever scold me.

She was so good that whatever she asked, you had to do it for her. Not only I, but my three sisters did the same thing. We could never refuse her because she herself went out of the way to help us all the time. She never said "no" to us.

When she died, mobs and mobs of people came to the funeral and we never expected it. She loved every person she met. What a winning personality! All of my friends, everyone, loved her.

She was the real guiding light in the family.

She was so very giving. I'd come home, get undressed and throw my shoes and clothes all over the place. She'd follow me and pick up, never with a harsh word.

My father was the opposite, "Now you do it or else...!" I'd defy him and then run to get behind my mother for protection.

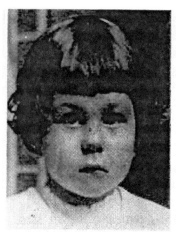

Lester in 1912—age 2½.

Lester in 1918—age 9.

Lester in 1926—age 16—his high school graduation picture.

When I became a teen-ager and was dating girls, she gently said, "Just be careful, Lester. Just be careful."

I said, "Don't worry, Mom. I know what I'm doing." I thought I was a man.

***

I was a bewildered, quiet, small child, always down at the end of the line in school because of my shortness. My predominate characteristic was shyness.

It's a horrible thing being shy. In first grade when I was supposed to recite a Christmas poem, my mother was so delighted, she diligently helped me learn it. I was trying not to, but I did learn it only to make her happy. Then I got sick the day of the Christmas party. I really played sick.

I did the same thing through high school and college. I never got up in front of the class. I was always out sick on days of oral compositions when I would have had to speak to the class. Even when the teacher called my name, I'd blush and blush and feel incapacitated.

When I'd blush, people would say, "Look, he's blushing!" I would turn redder and redder and I would want to die.

Even after college, if I'd see a girl I liked coming down the street, I'd walk around the block to avoid passing her, even if I were on the other side of the street. I used to die when approaching a girl I liked.

Yet I was able to force it, eventually, slowly, and the shyness would go away with that particular girl.

I was extremely withdrawn and introspective as a child, wondering what this life was all about. It never added up. I never felt as though I belonged to my family, to society. I could never understand the why of life itself. It never made any sense to me. I felt like a stranger in this world. That feeling I could never get away from.

Maybe it was a sense of not being in the right place?

But I tried to fit in. I tried to do what was right. I tried to be as I was expected to be, as everyone else was.

But I was always bewildered. I always wanted to know the why's and just had no answers to them.

My father was a tall, very good-looking, egotistical fellow, nattily dressed all the time. He was not the intellectual type; he was interested in the usual goals of the world. My mother, on the other hand, was always interested in culture. When I was a kid, she'd take me to shows and museums in New York City. But dad stayed home.

She took me to Broadway shows, musicals and Barnum and Bailey Circuses. I guess it was her way of introducing me to culture and fun.

My parents wanted me to be a doctor or a lawyer. My father used to brag all the time about me, except if I were present. Then he'd switch to the opposite. It was silly.

My father was very emotional; he would hug and kiss me in public, even when I was in my twenties. I thought it un-masculine and used to hate it. He was very warm and emotional that way.

My parents were not really religious, but my grandfathers on both sides were holy people, rabbis. I've seen pictures of my great-grandfathers, very aristocratic and distinguished looking rabbis.

My grandfather left Russia to avoid having his sons pulled into the army. He bought a passport with the name Levenson on it. That's how I got my name. It was originally Prehonnica.

I have three sisters: Florence, a year and a half older than I, Doris, five years younger, and Naomi, ten years younger.

My father favored Florence, She would tease me and start a fight and I would always get blamed for it. I couldn't do anything about it,

But with my younger sisters I always got along beautifully. When my father passed on, I really became their father and took care of the family.

My kid sister has been like a baby to me always. Now she's a grandmother, but to me she's still the baby. I can now understand why eighty-year-old parents treat their sixty-year-old children like kids.

Our family was always close. My sisters and I used to meet after dates, around the refrigerator in the kitchen, one, two, three in the morning and talk for hours.

So it was a friendly group.

My father was a businessman. He had about half a dozen workers, and this was before the days of the A & P and chain stores.

We always lived a little better than most of the people around us. My father was never rich, though. In fact, during my adult life, he was usually in debt. The A & P put him out of the grocery business.

Then in my 20's my father went into real estate, pyramiding, owning lots of land everywhere. But in 1929, with the financial crack-up, he lost all that and eventually even the house we were living in.

But in 1930 he opened up a luncheonette. Actually it was a stationery store, but I introduced sandwiches and coffee and it became more successful as a luncheonette.

The luncheonette was the center of the family until the sudden passing away of my mother because of pneumonia. My father never got over it. He became ill and for a year and a half gradually withered away from pining for our lost mother.

When my father passed on, my uncle wanted me to say the very sacred and holy prayer that you say for the dead. I looked him right in the eyes and said, "Will it bring him back? If it does, I'll say it."

He just turned away.

I didn't say the prayer because I didn't think it would.

When my father passed on, I sort of became the father of the family. My youngest sister, Naomi, was in high school. Doris was already out of it, and Florence had begun teaching, She was really on her own.

And so, I took over as head of the household and ran the luncheonette. When I took over, it was ten thousand dollars indebt because of my father's illness.

And because it wasn't doing very well, I held onto my job as an air conditioning engineer. I really worked around the clock keeping that place going.

My father left us with heavy debts. Wanting to uphold the honor of the family, I was determined to pay them off. So I did a few little things to the store and it started making money. Within a year's time, I had the debts taken care of.

After my mother died, I missed her so much I couldn't sleep the first year. At the time, I thought grieving was the right thing to do. Now I know it was nothing but selfishness. I wanted the comfort of her being around me, to give me the love she used to give me. I missed the affection she had been giving me.

At that time I believed there was no life after death. Nothing was real except that which you could feel, sense, touch and prove right in front of your eyes. My beloved mother had become dust.

LOVE IS LOVING THE OTHER ONE BECAUSE THE OTHER ONE IS THE WAY HE OR SHE IS

When I was a child the streets in Elizabeth were mostly unpaved dirt. Only the main street was paved with cobblestones. Horses and wagons were the way of transportation. Electricity wasn't in yet. We had gaslights, although all my neighborhood friends had homes with kerosene lamps.

My father took us out riding Sundays by hitching the horse to the surrey. People worked twelve hours a day, six days a week. But they were friendlier. Come Sunday, we had picnics or would visit.

There was very little entertainment so people would get together for fun. It seemed a nicer way of life than today.

There were no radio, television or movies. I first remember movies around 1918. It cost 5 cents to see Pearl White, Tom Mix and all those serials.

I built a radio in about 1920, when radio was in its infancy. I was in high school. I got an oatmeal box and wound some wire on it, put on a slide tuner, added a crystal and a pair of earphones, and to my surprise it worked. The first song I heard was "Tomorrow, Tomorrow, How Happy I Will Be." It was such a thrill that I never forgot it.

I always liked science and mechanics. I was always playing around up in the attic where I had an electronic lab, always experimenting with little gadgets.

As a child I'd take everything apart in the house. I'd take the clocks apart and usually get them working again with a few extra parts left over.

I was probably nine or ten years old when I took apart the player piano. I just got it together in time before my father got home.

I remember once taking the steel spring out of the victrola, and boy! What a job getting it back! Took me days, but they didn't use the thing so I got away with it. With extreme, unusual forcing, I finally got that heavy steel spring back into its place and the victrola worked again.

My parents knew my tendency and I was always being warned: Don't touch!

The first clock didn't work when I put it back together.

I remember being caught at something else.

I was nine years old. I was told I could have anything I wanted in the store. That led me to taking cigarettes.

It was the kids in the gang who encouraged me. I used to take a pack of Luckies. Then we shifted to Camels.

We'd gather at night up in the hayloft, my father's hayloft for the horses, and would we be big shots, smoking away. We even tried cigars one Saturday and after the smoke we went swinging on the swing below the hayloft. The awful sickness and nausea that resulted finished any more interest in cigars. I was so sick that my mother couldn't help noticing, although I was trying to hide it. I fought her calling a doctor for fear he would know I was smoking cigars.

I once gave a cigarette to Doris. Doris was only four years old. She asked for it and I said, "Sure," and I gave it to her.

This was in the kitchen. I didn't know my father was around.

She took a big puff, breathed it in, and coughed and coughed and coughed. And just as she started to cough, in walked my father! Oh! Did I get it! Did he yell!

I scrammed. I left the house because I felt that this was going to be catastrophic.

In those days no good women smoked. It was really considered an evil thing to do. And you certainly did not give a four year old girl a cigarette.

In my elementary school days parents were so busy making a living that we were on our own. When we came home from school, the first thing we'd do would be to get on the street and meet the gang. With a broomstick as a bat, and a piece of it cut off a caddy, we'd play ball. We'd also use tin cans to play duck-on-the-rock and other games devised by our ingenuity. There was real good camaraderie amongst kids in those days.

We were fortunate in not being smothered by parental over-attention. We better learned to take care of ourselves, an advantage we had over kids today.

I remember getting a bicycle for myself.

At the age of ten I prayed to God every night for a bicycle for half a year. But the bicycle didn't come. I wanted it so badly. I went into much thought. I realized I could get a job delivering newspapers and maybe buy one myself. I did get a job. At 50 cents a week the money didn't accumulate very fast, but it got me my first bicycle- a five dollar, beat-up, second hand one.

***

My mother, a great pacifist, taught me early that it's always better to run from a fight than it is to fight. It was an awful thing to teach me, because in those days the kids

141

were cruel and would gang up on me because I was a Jew and was small.

One day I was on the ground with five of them punching away at me. I couldn't take it any longer and lost my temper. I began furiously punching back. They started to run, and I was chasing five of them!

I stopped suddenly and took a look. I said, "Oh my God! I used to die of fear of them and here they are, *five of them, running away from me!*" I resolved, "Never again will I show any fear." I was nine years old and in the third grade at the time. That lesson never left me.

We moved around quite a lot during my school days. As soon as I'd enroll in a new school I knew from experience that the school bully was going to challenge me because I was a little Jew-boy. So I would quickly challenge the bully and scare him to the point where we wouldn't have to fight. I was scared but I learned how to hide my fear. However, as time went on, my fears actually diminished because assuming fearlessness taught me fearlessness.

In 1952, through my realizations, I lost *all* fear. How nice that is!

I don't think I ever had any spiritual experiences when I was a boy. If anything, I was very much against all that nonsense.

In fact, I was strongly anti-religious. I even fought my parents on it, especially my father with his ideas of dietary law. I upset the kosherism of the house because I thought it nonsense.

We had a maid, and I got her to buy steaks at a non-kosher butcher store. Kosher steaks, being fresh, were tough, like leather. The non-kosher steaks were aged and tender.

As my father ate he remarked how great the steaks were. I said, "You like them?"

He said, "They're excellent."

"Well," I said, "they're not kosher." He gave me a look and I thought he was going to tear me apart. He didn't say a word, he was so furious. But he didn't stop eating the steaks.

I shouldn't have done that. It showed the rebel in me at times.

The only reason we kept a kosher house was that my grandfather lived nearby. My grandfather and great-grandfather were holy, orthodox men.

I was given the usual early religious training until I was twelve.

When I entered college and began some deep thinking on that religious training I thought, "Gee, how they fooled me!" I rebelled and went into a complete reversal, I was so anti-religious I used to mock God.

I remember once saying to my orthodox grandfather, "You cannot prove your God exists. What makes you believe in God?" And he answered, "All my life I have believed in Him. Now, near the end, should I take the chance of not believing?" This made me aware of his broadmindedness and his love for me.

LOVE IS TAKING PEOPLE AS THEY ARE

The only person I really spoke to intimately while I was in high school was Simon, a friend who was way beyond me in years. He taught at Rutgers University in Newark, the next town, and I really looked up to him as a guide.

You couldn't talk philosophically to a fellow of your own age. I was way beyond my years in what I was reading and studying. At grammar school I was studying books from my father's aborted medical career. And in high school I was reading psychology, economics and philosophy. So by the time I hit college, I was very deep into all these things.

Simon really led me into the heart of all philosophies—Kant, Hegel, Schopenhauer—I can't remember the other ones but I read them all very studiously and I understood them. We were also very interested in Freud and so we studied in a very intense manner—much better than you would in college—philosophy, psychology, and economics, both of us seeking answers.

He never got them. He thought the answer was economics until he eventually saw it wasn't.

But he was a guiding light for many, many years through high school, college and post-college days.

He's the one who liked camping and led me into it. We would spend the summer in the Catskill Mountains and occasionally in the Adirondack Mountains of New York State. We had a beautiful community life of campers—quite a variation of types there. We had Mr. Coar who was a minister, a reverend. And we had Jack, the taxicab driver, who was a real New York City rebel activist. And then there were others.

Each one would set up his own camp for himself and maybe one other, and in the evenings we'd get together around the campfire. We'd make our favorite, what we called slum galleon. We'd get a big two-and-a-half gallons washing pail - and throw everything into it, beans, meats, salamis, spices, onions, vegetables and hot dogs. It would cook for hours and hours. And it really was delicious.

And often, after everyone went to bed, Simon and I would talk deep into the night. We talked about all the philosophies and the "why's" of life. We discussed mainly the two major philosophical schools of idealism and materialism. We rejected agnosticism as getting nowhere. Then, I thought philosophy was the greatest means of understanding. Now, I see philosophy as nothing more than going in circles with words, since you do not get understanding of life.

Materialism appealed to me then. The other seemed silly. I built such a beautiful, solid, concrete, materialistic philosophy that I thought it was unshakable. I could prove to you anything I would say. It was like the law of gravity. I'd hold a pencil and keep dropping it. It worked all the time. I'd say, "This is the law of gravity. Now prove to me your God. You can't. Therefore there is no God. It's nonsense."

In high school I became the intellectual type, interested in books and the so-called better things of life. Music interested me, especially jazz. I taught myself how to play piano. I could really play jazz. I could hear a tune and then play it.

I was good in all sports. I played handball and tennis with the top winners in high school and college. And I could beat them, as long as it wasn't a competition. Competitively, I was no good. So I could never be on the teams.

I graduated from High School in 1925. I was an honor student but always had the weird feeling every time I took an exam that I was going to fail. Instead I'd come out with the highest marks. This went on for 12 years! What anxiety and sweat I would go through before an exam. That was how little I thought of myself. Isn't that what an inferiority complex is?

My marks in math and science, without studying, were always in the 90's. English and history I would just struggle through with 80's. I had no interest in them.

Anyone is smart in any subject he is interested in; anyone is dumb in any subject he is not interested in.

In high school, even though I had this inferiority complex which made me think myself unattractive, the girls used to say, "Oh, isn't he cute."

It's a funny thing to go through life being one way, and feeling the opposite all the time. The girls thought I was good-looking; I thought I wasn't. I habitually belittled of myself.

I was intensely sexed and my whole life centered around sex. Wanting women made me with tremendous effort break through my shyness. I used to scheme, "How can I get them?" It was through observing that I learned how to get the women I wanted.

And it worked out beautifully.

I used to watch what the other fellows did. I'd notice what the girls did and didn't like. The other fellows would throw out compliments so loosely that the girls knew it was just flattery and not real. I saw that the girls liked compliments. Every girl had nice things about her. So I complimented them, but only on the things that were really true.

Also, I noticed that boys talked a lot about themselves; the girls didn't like that. They liked to be talked about. So I didn't talk about myself; I talked about them.

These things always gave me the girl I wanted. Always.

I knew how to make a play for a girl and win; this, in spite of the tremendous obstacle of shyness. After establishing rapport, then the shyness was no longer an obstacle; it was an asset. Girls loved it!

I looked up to, worshiped and idolized women, and therefore couldn't have anything to do with a prostitute, or some girl picked up on the street. I could never understand my college fraternity brothers saying they wouldn't dare touch their girlfriends – but they would go to bed with strange girls they picked up on the street, who in no way compared with their girls friends.

Do you know why the fellows did that? That's what they thought of sex.

To me, sex was made for the girl you loved. That was so natural!

Sex brought out the finest emotions in me. I had the highest respect for women. Wanting to protect their reputations, I would never tell anyone of my affairs. In those days, for an unmarried woman, having sex was committing the unpardonable sin.

Basically, sex brought out my finer feelings of love and really made me a giving person.

During those days, when people asked me if I believed in God, would say, "Yes." And when they would ask, "What is your concept of God?" I would say, "Sex!" On their surprise I would explain that it brought out in me the noblest and finest of human feelings, and that nothing could bring out these feelings as well as sex could.

Later I discovered that sex pegs your joy at a certain level and keeps you from increasing your joy. I've reached a state where now I always have more joy than what sex can give at its best. There is no limit to the joy that one may experience.

Even in grammar school I was always madly in love. In every grade I fell in love with one beautiful girl. I remember the first one, Marcella Higgins in the first grade, Marcella Kahn in the second, Ethel Solomon in the third, and so on. Although I was so intensely enamored of them, they never knew it.

Ethel Solomon was seated right across the aisle from me, and every time she looked at me, I turned red. I almost died every time she spoke to me.

You can see what a torturous life I lived.

During my adolescent years, we had many parties. The fellows were always crude and forward with the girls, so the girls ran away from them to me for protection, because I was nice!

Because of my shyness, I was never forceful with them—just the opposite. I really wanted to protect them, enjoying the pleasant feeling of being their hero.

Through protecting them, we got involved. It was natural.

I had sex all my life, never really promiscuously, but with many. I never cared to have more than one at a time. I wanted love with the girls I went to bed with.

***

I was in love and kept going with Annette in high school and half way through college.

We had a good, healthy, natural sex relationship, the way it should be when two people are in love. When you're a teen-ager, sex is very intense.

I was going to Rutgers in New Brunswick, New Jersey while she was going to the University of Pennsylvania. We couldn't see each other because of the distance. She started dating other fellows and over the phone she told me about it.

I was so extremely jealous it was tearing my insides apart. I couldn't take it. I almost flunked out that third year in college. I had to take a re-exam in my major. It was one term only, so I still made honors.

When I started college, dormitories were few, and I was rooming far off campus. Being against the idea of fraternities with their exclusiveness, I avoided them. However, the inconveniences of off-campus living were great. So I finally moved into a fraternity house, right on campus.

Living there gave me a very balanced collegiate life. I was a good student and also participated in all the social activities, attended all athletic events – even followed the football team around—and was very active in handball, tennis and swimming.

I loved college. It gave me avenues of freedom that made it easier for a shy person like myself to move into the world.

You suddenly become a man when you entered college. You moved out of being treated like a child in your family into your own home, your fraternity house.

I was a man and we were men talking about important, bug-time worldly subjects. Oh, we were smart! We knew more than our professors knew!

We talked about the world and women, and played cards often until the sun came up. Then we'd go to bed to get up an hour or two before eight o'clock class.

I remember the glamour of college in those days. "Rah, Rah, Rutgers! I'll die for dear old Rutgers!" The whole thing was Hollywoodian naïve, fairytalelish!

At the time, usually only the sons of rich men went to college. I never considered myself one of them. Although my father started me, I had to finish by working my way through.

I went to work during the third year of college when I got a letter, which said, "Dear Lester, I can't send any more money. Love, Dad." The Depression had broken him financially.

I thought that my world had come to an end, as I equated my college education with my world. I even considered suicide, which was a thought that would reoccur to me on occasions until 1952.

It took me three days to figure out I could work my way through college! Immediately I got a dual job in the fraternity house in which I was living, washing dishes and stoking the coal furnace. That partly took care of me. A few months later, I managed to get a real position as a laboratory assistant in the physics department.

I always felt poor. Compared to the other fellows, I was. My roommate's father was a millionaire – in the thirties. But it didn't bother me that they were rich. It bothered me that I felt poor.

We didn't differentiate in the fraternity house. We were all frat brothers, and naturally we worked for one another. We felt like one happy family, freed from parental oppression.

I rebelled against compulsory daily chapel.

We had to go to chapel every day. Some of the fellows would take decks of cards and play while the poor chaplain gave the sermon. There was so much talking that no one could hear him. I felt sorry for him. But we won our point; chapel was made Sundays only, and voluntary.

They were giving us the usual organized religious teaching, which doesn't go far enough. When you are in college and you're young, you are thinking, and you can see how silly the stuff is they're pouring out to you.

Rebellion came out in our day also in the form of our dress. We wore raccoon coats and derby hats! What an odd combination. But such things always went on, and go on today.

Youth always objects.

Military training was compulsory and I protested it. I was anti-military, and was the worst soldier in the worst company.

We were given old World War I uniforms. They were heavy wool and itchy. My jacket was too small and my pants were too big. With my jacket buttoned, I could just about breathe. My pants looked like bloomers. My boyish-looking hat sat on top of my head. I looked like a real Hollywood comic.

In a way I liked this comic dress. It fitted in with my attitude about the military.

Drill was where I could express the way I felt. I'd play dumb. They'd command, "Right, march!" and I'd go left.

One time at drill our officer, a recent graduate of West Point, wanted to give us a rest. He had us stack our rifles and went into a speech emphasizing the point of not going near the stacked arms: "Stay away from the arms. When you break ranks, don't move through the stacks. Move back away from them. Stay away from them. And remember, don't touch the arms!"

As he said that, I instinctively put my arm out to touch a stack, thinking he wouldn't see me. But at that moment his head swung around and he saw me touch it. I quickly pulled my hand back. But unfortunately, the stack of rifles had been wrongly stacked, and down it went, hitting the next stack, which hit the next one.

Did the officer have it in for me! He was so furious that he huffed and he puffed. He just couldn't say a word to me.

I got a big share of demerits for that.

The two West Point graduates who were in charge called me in for a conference after the second year, at the end of the course. They told me they were going to flunk me. They said that although my class marks were in the 90's, my drill work had so many demerits I would have to take the last year over again.

I thought. Then I pointed my finger at them and said, "Okay, remember. You fellows flunk me, and you're going to have me another year!"

They looked at each other and said, "You're passed!"

152

I was a wise guy. I knew the military wouldn't do anything to me in peacetime. They didn't have a guardhouse!

LOVE AND UNDERSTANDING
ARE THE SAME

I graduated from Rutgers in 1931 at the age of twenty-two.

I wanted to be the greatest physicist in the world, but I couldn't get a job. The very few physicists working in those days had been laid off. Still I felt as though I was going to conquer the world. I never let up seeking work. I was turned down day in and day out, but I never stopped looking.

Since I couldn't get a job as a physicist, I decided to go into engineering. Physics was the basis for all engineering, and as extra study I had taken electrical and mechanical engineering. I had also taken the required educational courses to qualify for a teaching certificate.

So I came out of college qualified for several things.

My first job with an aeronautical engineer lasted only three months because he went out of business.

Then I looked for work as a teacher.

Jobs being so hard to get, I would go every day to the superintendent of schools and ask him for a job. Week in and week out, I was doing this, until one day – I believe in order to get rid of me – he gave me a job substituting for a man who had a class of incorrigibles. These boys had already been expelled from school for having done violent things, and were on their way to reform school. This class was an attempt to bring some of them back into the school system, rather than send them on to reform school.

Wanting a job so badly, I was happy to be given this work. However, on the way into the school (Jacques Street School, Number Nine) I met the supervisor of the physical education for the city, Mr. Allison, my old gym teacher from Battin High. When I told him where I was headed, he said, "Don't go there. If I were you, I wouldn't do it. Yesterday they took the substitute teacher before you, and actually threw him over the fence. And he's bigger than you. Stay away."

I was so determined and so wanting work, I said, "I'll try it anyway." With my learned fearlessness, I dared the assignment.

I walked into the class—they were in their carpentry shop—and it was pandemonium. One kid was sawing his desk in half, another was chopping plaster out of the wall with a hammer, and every other one was doing anything and everything he wanted to do.

So I went up to the boy sawing his desk in half and told him to stop it. He just looked at me and turned around as if I weren't there.

I went to the boy chopping the plaster out of the wall and asked him to stop. He answered, "Go to hell!"

I went to the front of the class, picked up a plank – a four-inch-wide plank about three feet long -- and yelled out, like a thunder clap, "Quiet!"

No one paid any attention, except for just a moment.

I went to the fellow sawing his desk in half, hit him, and he stopped.

Then I went for the fellow who was chopping the plaster out of the wall and he started running, but I caught him in the back. I didn't hurt him much.

What I was doing got me the attention of the class. So I went back to the front of the class, and again yelled, "Quiet!" Then something started that I was concerned might happen: the leader of the class, stood up and said, "Okay boys, let him"... and before he could say the words "have it" I went for him. With both my hands on the plank, I came down over his head and he fell back into his seat, stunned. Fortunately, the plank broke in half, which allowed me a better grip on it.

Then I went for a second fellow who had moved to join him. He started to run away. But I swung at him and cut four of his fingers. For me it was do or die. I was really in there, ready to take on the whole class.

From that spot, I yelled, "Okay! Who's next?" Then as a group, the whole class sat down in their seats. They submitted to my challenge and became absolutely quiet.

I then opened the door and soon Miss Kellog, the principal, peeked in. She looked stunned. I said, "Come in, Miss Kellog." When she did, she couldn't talk. She had expected to find me in pieces, but I was fine and the kids were perfectly still. I said "Everything is fine." She stuttered something and walked out, a little dazed.

This all happened in the first minutes of my coming into the class. For the rest of the week I had excellent rapport with the boys, much more than I believed, because at the end of the last day with the class I said to them, "Mr. Peters will be back tomorrow," and they all exclaimed in unison, "Aw-w-w." I said, "What's the matter?"

"Oh, we like you. We wish you'd stay!"

This puzzled me at first. Then I realized the reason for it was I was talking to them in the language they understood. I was talking to them at their level. I was not hitting them out of blood-thirstiness. I didn't even want to hit them.

I had guts and they liked that. I was able to communicate better than I realized because I understood them. I was given the job of being the leader, the teacher. They were challenging it. I took the challenge and showed them that I could be the leader. This they understood and this they accepted, and this they liked.

I was telling them, "Look, this is my job. I've been given the position of leader here. You fellows shouldn't, and can't, take it away from me. If you do, I'll do whatever is necessary to re-establish my leadership."

You couldn't have a class unless you were with it, unless you had a feel for it, unless you had a love for your pupils. A teacher who had hatred for the class couldn't control it.

Because of my ability to communicate, the kids were with me. I got the reputation of being a good disciplinarian. I was told I would lose my job if I hit the kids, but I did it anyway. It was necessary, I thought, for control.

It's interesting how my students reacted. I once lost my temper and swung a blackboard pointer at a boy as he was running away. I caught him across the forehead and forearm, and he developed two welts.

The next day in school he came to me and said, "Gee, Mr. Levenson, my old man beat the hell outta me, wanting me to tell him who did this to me. But I wouldn't."

He protected me.

That wild experience with the thirty "incorrigible" boys earned me respect and my first regular teaching assignment. I taught geometry to juniors and seniors in the high school from which I had graduated. Bettin High school had been made an all girls school. I was twenty-two, teaching girls who were eighteen. It was humiliating.

Because of my extreme shyness, the girls would tease me by coming up after class and crowding around me, pushing against me. I'd squirm, and they knew I was squirming.

Some would sit purposely letting their dresses go above their knees. And I'd have to look away.

I used to walk home from school, as I lived only a half mile away. Some of the girls with bikes would slow down and shout to me, "Yoo-hoo, would you like to have a ride?"

"No, thank you," I'd say, hoping the principal or no other teacher saw it.

Jobs being very scarce, I wanted to hold that position. I couldn't risk having the principle or anyone else see anything that didn't look perfectly respectable for a teacher.

At the end of the teaching year, the teacher that I had replaced returned and I was sent to a junior high school in the poorest section of Elizabeth port, New Jersey. I was given the most difficult kids, the group with the lowest I.Q.s.

It was a weird thing, that experience of teaching. In a way I was rough with the kids, but I never had the attitude that I was their superior. I dealt with them person to person. My attitude was one of understanding them and what they were doing. And they were behaving accordingly. Understanding and love are the same.

They certainly protected me. They could have me thrown out of the school system again and again for hitting them, and they knew it. But they never did.

You see, it is not what you do but your attitude as you do it that counts.

During the second year of teaching I grew tired of it and quit. It was dull. I wanted to be a scientist. There were no jobs. I was frustrated and confused. I felt heavy, heavy all over.

ONE DOES NOT INCREASE ONE'S LOVE
ONE MERELY GETS RID OF ONE'S HATE

About the middle of the depression I had no job, so I went camping for the summer. I loved camping. It was the nicest recreation I knew. For many years, working or not, I'd take the summer off and go camping. I'd just throw a piece of canvas and bed under it. I usually camped with one or two others.

We caught fish by hand. Belly-tickling, it was called. It was illegal, but the fastest way of catching fish. I'd feel under the rocks for speckled brook trout. While under the rock, the fish thinks that your hand is part of the environment floating by, and feels safe. Once I made contact, I worked my hand up toward the fish's head, grabbed it tightly, and quickly threw it on the bank as it was slipping out of my grasp.

But there was a twenty-five dollar fine for each fish, so we'd fish in twos. One of us would watch out for the game warden. Each time we'd catch a fish, we'd hide it and get another one. In a matter of minutes, we got a meal together that way.

I loved to live naturally. We tried to live off the land, eating apples and berries that grew wild in the Catskills and the corn, vegetables and milk farmers sometimes gave us. We even drank milk warm from the cow, although it had an odor thinking that was natural.

My camping was an escape from the world. Every time I'd go camping, in a day or two all my pains and ulcers would disappear; when I'd get back to the city in a few days, my sicknesses would return.

***

I had an unconscious fear of getting tied up in marriage that was so strong it prevented me from ever marrying. Because I felt so bound up all the time I feared marriage would put a big increase on that non-freedom I was feeling.

I tried once to force marriage with an awfully nice girl from Elizabeth. It was toward the beginning of World War II. President Roosevelt had signed the draft act. I though, "Well, I might go to war and be killed. I should get married and leave some offspring."

So I said to Selma point blank, "Would you like to get married?"

"Yes!" she said.

I said, "okay, would you go down to the state of Virginia with me right now?"

She said, "Yes."

So we took off for Virginia where you can get married right away. All the way down I couldn't talk. After driving a couple of hours, I swallowed hard and with a gulp asked, "Are you hungry?"

And she said, "Yes."

"Okay, let's eat."

Throughout the meal I couldn't talk. I felt as though I were Atlas with the whole weight of the world on my back. But I was determined to go through with it.

We crossed the Virginia state line and stopped at the first place with a sign "Marriages Performed Immediately."

A minister came out and said, "Oh, you'd like to get married? Fine."

When he said, "Fine," I blacked out for a moment.

Then he said, "Now, you have to take a place in town and stay three days before I can do this. The new law requires that."

"Oh in that case, I can't wait because I must be back for work." It really was no excuse, it blurted out uncontrolled. On saying it I felt as though the world had rolled off my back.

I just couldn't go through with it.

On the way home not a word was said.

After this incident I never saw Selma again. I was too ashamed. I wanted to see her. But I just couldn't.

The marriage obstacle was unconscious then. Now, of course, I know what it was. I wanted freedom so much that I couldn't allow myself to tie to marriage.

TO LOVE OUR ENEMY IS
THE HEIGHT OF LOVE

I decided to go abroad and escape from my unhappy world. The Depression was on and everything was so difficult. I was terribly unhappy and frustrated at the way my life was working out.

One hundred and twenty-five dollars bought me a roundtrip ticket to Liverpool, England, and launched me on a period of freedom from my inner extreme frustration, tension and anxieties. I spent most of the time abroad in Helsinki.

It was such an ideal, quiet, clean city! And the rate of exchange was so favorable. I'd get hundreds of their marks for one dollar. On three dollars a week, I had everything I needed.

For that period I just lived. I had saved enough money from teaching.

I did nothing but observe. The nicest thing was the escape from me and my miseries. Here I was in a strange country, strange ways, language—everything was different. It fascinated me and incidentally broadened me. I saw that what was right conduct in one country was often wrong in another. This taught me greater acceptance of all peoples and their ways. I believed I gained more of a practical knowledge of living and people by traveling than I had learned in four years of college.

I personally felt that traveling was the very nicest way of entertaining myself. Next to traveling, it was camping out in nature.

Even in Europe I always found a girl, and lived similarly to my life in America.

I came back from Europe in 1935 and sought a job as an air conditioning engineer. I thought air conditioning was the coming thing. It was just starting about that time. I applied for a job and was told by Kelvinator that they didn't need another engineer. I told them I'd work for nothing, and actually offered my services free.

They started me and in a week or two paid me fifteen dollars a week. It didn't take long before I was getting fifty dollars a week. For that time it was excellent pay. I soon tired of the work and quit before the year was up. I figured out that I could sell at Kelvinator's cost and make their mark by going into business on my own. I used the address and phone number of a friend who was clerking in a legal office. My office was in my hat. I was my own salesman, engineer, installation man, electrician and service man.

The first job I installed in 1937 in the Red Cross shoe store was still operating in 1973. When I put the job in, I did it in the way I knew would be the very best. I slowed the fan and slightly over-sized the equipment. I knew it would last.

When I was selling the job, the storeowner asked, "How do I know this is going to work? Two thousand dollars is a lot of money, you know."

I had an idea. I said, "If it doesn't work, you don't pay me! Just let me put it in, but sign the contract now."

I knew that with his signature I could borrow money from the bank next door.

I installed it, it worked and he paid me for it.

That started me off in the air conditioning business. I discovered I could work four months a year and make more than I made as an engineer working a whole year.

That was at the time my father died and left a luncheonette business with a ten-thousand-dollar debt. So I ran the air conditioning business and the luncheonette at the same time. I just wanted to pay off the family debts and dump the luncheonette. That's what I did.

I was restless and bored. I thought I would hit the big town, New York City. I dropped New Jersey and went to New York in 1938 with a smart idea. I opened up a very small and efficient luncheonette called the Hitching Post. It was the smallest restaurant in New York, so said a newspaper—eleven seats, around a circular counter.

I designed the counter out of ash wood and an old craftsman from Germany hand made the stools. They were beautiful. So much more beautiful that the usual chrome and red plastic furniture of those days. The walls were mahogany. The whole place had a natural air of wood, with a fireplace in the corner.

I really engineered the food business. I was able to get the prices very low and the percentage profits very high.

We sold a hot roast beef sandwich on a warm soft roll dipped in natural gravy for ten cents, and a hot Virginia ham sandwich on a warm soft roll dipped in natural gravy for ten cents. Our homemade buttercrust apple pie was baked on the premises, and a la mode or with a slice of cheese, the price was ten cents. The pie was really delicious.

Although these prices were very low, the percentage profit was much higher than at the majority of eating places.

By 1941 I had three Hitching Post restaurants going and a fourth was under way. I was making twelve hundred dollars a week and, at the time, living in the Hotel Taft on Broadway, New York City.

I used to work twelve to fourteen hours a day—around the clock—seven days a week. I always worked long hours, for two reasons: first because I always started in business with no money; second, I needed the difficult involvement to escape from my turbulent, unhappy mind.

Then the war interfered.

In July 1941 I was called in as an engineer for the U.S. Maritime Commission in Washington, D.C. They needed ships to deliver the war material to England. I worked in the engineering plan approval division, on ships piping and machinery.

From the start of this job, I thought of leaving it and returning full time to the restaurant. However, I was locked into my job. Because of the war, I could not leave my employment. I was considered necessary to the war effort so they sent a providential deferment to my draft brand.

Every Saturday afternoon at 1 P.M. I left Washington for New York, to look after the Hitching Posts; every Sunday night at 7 P.M. I'd drive back to Washington, 470 long miles, roundtrip.

But I couldn't operate them from afar, and I lost all the Hitching Post restaurants.

At the Maritime Commission I was surprised to meet strong anti-Semitism amongst my fellow engineers.

When I first walked into the Commission, an elderly engineer said, "Come here." I walked over to him. He asked me if I were a Jew. When I told him, he said, "Well I hate all Jews."

"Why?" I asked.

"Well, all Jews are crooks," he answered.

"Are you calling me a crook?" I asked.

"Well all <u>Brooklyn</u> Jews are crooks," he replied. So I answered,

"I come from Brooklyn," although I really didn't. He just turned away and wouldn't talk to me any more.

That was my introduction to the Maritime Commission. My blood used to boil when confronted with anti-Semitism but I suppressed the anger, at least outwardly.

At another time one of my co-workers, came up to me and said, "Oh, I got this at one of *your* stores."

I said, "What do you mean?" I didn't have any stores in Washington.

"I got gypped." He said.

"One of my stores?" I inquired again.

"You know, I bought it in a Jew-store."

That was the way it went, again and again with my fellow engineers.

While working for Kelvinator as an engineer in 1936, the senior engineer said to me one day, "You know Lester, before I met you I thought all Jews and niggers were the same. But now I think the Jews are a little better."

These are not special incidents. This sort of thing went on all my life until I gained my freedom and realized that I was responsible for everything that was happening to me. That's when it stopped.

I was beat up when I was a kid for being a Jew. In high school I was often ostracized and attacked. In college I joined a Jewish fraternity. The fellows in the non-Jewish fraternity across the street with whom I played touch football wouldn't talk to me if they met me at a college dance.

I got this king of treatment continuously all my life until 1952. I'd hear remarks all the time, everywhere, on the streets. I was never away from it.

When jobs were extremely scarce and I needed work, I was first accepted and then turned down by the Manhattan Project because I was a Jew. That was the project to develop the atomic bomb. I never was sorry about that one.

I was classified 2B. Humorously, I though that means to be here when they go and to be here when they come back.

2B meant essential to the war effort. Engineers especially were needed. So that got me a deferment right through the war, although I was tied as tightly as any man in uniform. All my bosses were in uniform and were either generals or near-generals. I had no freedom to move around. I had to go where they sent me. So in a way it was like being in the Army without being in a uniform.

When I saw some of my fellow workers, who also had deferments, being drafted, I thought, "Well, one of these days I'll have to go."

But I couldn't get myself to the place where I could kill. I just felt that I could never kill a man.

But then I said, "Well, I'll have to kill. I might get to the front line." So I began training myself so that in case I was drafted, I'd be able to kill. I used to read all the Nazi atrocities to the Jews and I'd imagine myself as being one of them.

But even though I kept doing this for months, I still ended up with the feeling that I couldn't kill.

I said, "Well, if I have to go, maybe I'll close my eyes and do it."

In 1943 I was shifted to Philadelphia. There I got fed up with ships and pipes, and worked my way into the U.S. Engineers, working out of 120 Wall Street, getting up plans and specifications for construction at army installations. I had gotten back home to New York City! That was my plan.

By through all this period, I was sick mentally with anxieties and depression, sick physically with ulcers, hay fever, gastrointestinal imbalances and migraine headaches.

While in Washington I had began to develop fears of going under a bridge or into a building, thinking that they might collapse on me. Even though rationally I knew they couldn't, I couldn't get rid of the fear. I was forcing myself to go under railroad bridges.

This made me think I was going insane. And when you think you're going insane, you really get scared! It drove me to seek a way out. I went into the study of Freud with intensity.

Then I went into psychoanalysis. Four years of it – four times a week—under a former associate of Sigmund Freud. In 1946 I was discharged with the comment that some people cannot be helped.

It had done me no good.

WHEN ONE REALLY LOVES
ONE CAN NEVER BE HURT

When the war ended having been a Maritime
Engineer for two years and a construction engineer for

three I looked for a good business to get into. There was a dire shortage of homes, and lumber was hard to get. So I decided on the lumber business.

I never had money when I started a business. I always had to work on ideas. Money does not make money. Ideas make money.

A planing mill in Canada charges three dollars a thousand board feet; in the states, the cost was ten dollars. Seven dollars was the normal profit per thousand feet. That made a good business.

I got into my car and drove to Canada. For one dollar, I rented all the space around a planing mill in St. Raymond, about thirty miles out of Quebec City. In return, the owner of the planing mill would get all my business. I arranged for the saw millers to air-dry their timber there.

I got another fellow to work for me and handle the New York office, which was my apartment on 225 West 23rd Street. We'd sell the lumber in the New York- New Jersey area, and he'd take orders and take care of the customers.

In Canada I'd have the planing mill take the lumber from the stacks of drying lumber, send it through a belt line through the planer and into a railroad car.

The mill owner would seal the area, write out a bill of lading, hand it to me, and I would give him a check for the lumber and the planing of it.

I'd air mail the bill of lading to my man in New York. He'd run to the customers, get the customer's check, then deposit it to cover mine.

I got up to shipping two carloads of lumber a day and I was making three hundred dollars a carload. I could have made four or five hundred a carload, but I was satisfied with three.

Very early in this business, a customer left on vacation and was gone for several weeks. That could've wrecked me as I needed his check to cover mine for the two carloads I had just shipped to him. I always had good credit, but I was a stranger in Canada and one check bouncing would have ruined me. A carload average $2500 and I had a $5000 check that had to be covered.

I immediately took an airplane back to New York City and asked two or three banks for a loan to cover my lumber. They asked what security I had, and I told them —none. I didn't get the loan.

I had to cover that $5000 check or lose the business I'd just started. I remembered from the past how my confidence would flow over to the one I was speaking to. I figured I was lacking confidence. So I took two day off to develop it. I would bring up the feeling of confidence and strengthen this feeling until it just oozed out of me. Then I had it.

I walked into a strange bank, the Trade Bank and Trust Company, on Seventh and 34th Street. I knew they were dealing with the big lumber companies and I figured they'd understand lumber.

I wanted to see the president, but he was away on vacation. "Well, in that case," I said, "I'll see the VP."

They introduced me to him, the toughest guy in the bank. I knew I was going to get the loan. I never deviated from that.

He asked many questions and I answered them. "All right," he said, "Come in tomorrow. I think I'll give it to you."

I went in the next day and he started asking more questions. I could see he did not want to give me the loan.

He asked, "Did you say this?"

I said, "No, I said this." He was asking me about some very positive things that I had been thinking but had not voiced. I knew I had not said them. Yet he had picked them up! I thought it was very weird. To me mind reading was all nonsense in those days.

In the middle of his questioning he stood up, reached over, grabbed my hand in both of his and said, "Be careful, just be careful. I'm letting you have it."

My security for the loan was the invoice. I would invoice the customer, assign the invoice to the bank, and the bank would give me eighty per cent of the invoice, which covered all my costs. Ten thousand dollars credit was granted. That got me going again, just in time. It took about six to eight days to clear a check, and now my check was covered.

Here's another strange incident. One time I wanted to make a good buy in lumber and needed $4000 cash. I was in St. Raymond, Quebec at the time. I walked into the Royal Bank, wrote out a personal check for $4000 on my New York bank and handed it to the cashier to cash. She called over the manager and he asked me, "What do you want it for?"

"I want to buy lumber," I said.

He simply replied, "Okay," and gave me the cash. As I walked out of the bank I thought how weird this situation was—I, a stranger, was walking out of the door with $4000 cash in my pocket!

I went back and asked the manager why he had given me the cash so readily. I said, "You know I can walk out of this door and you could be out of $4000." He said, "I'm not afraid."

I said, shaking his hand vigorously, "Thank you." You're a hundred percent safe. You'll never be hurt." And I walked out.

As a stranger in a strange country—in a bank that I had not been in before—I wrote out a personal check for $4000. Trying to understand things like that used to give me a headache, so I would not think more about it. I said to myself, "The confidence in me goes over to him. But what makes him so trusting, I can not understand."

I always got credit and I always paid back.

As I was buying directly from saw millers and bypassing the Canadian brokers, it didn't take long for the brokers to gang up on me. I was the only American bypassing them and getting lumber they couldn't get. I paid the saw millers more, so I got first choice on the lumber.

I had started this way: I met a Canadian saw miller who had twelve or fourteen kids. I asked why he let his kids run around in the winter without shoes. He broke down and cried, and said he didn't earn enough money to buy his kids shoes. The Canadian brokers were cruel to the saw millers. They wouldn't let them make a living, even when lumber was as valuable as gold.

I told the miller that I'd give him three dollars more per thousand feet for his lumber. It was the normal profit he should have been making. After that, naturally, I got all the lumber I wanted from him and all the other saw millers.

I had accumulated about $80,000 worth of inventory when the Canadian brokers got after me.

They filed a charge against me for trying to leave the country while owing them $15,000. They did it late on a Friday afternoon, knowing that I wouldn't have time to get a bond before Monday.

The judge ordered me to jail until the bond was posted. I was so furious that I held on to the bars with such strength that the jailer couldn't push me into the cell. We were locked in a struggle.

A lawyer, who happened to be there, saw what was going on, felt sympathy for me, and vouched for me. I was released on his recognizance. After that I made him one of my attorneys.

While the court case was on, a stranger who worked in the court came up to me and said, "You know, you're going to win the case, but they're going to re-file the same charge for $50,000."

I quickly saw my lawyer, and he told me that I'd have to go to court for every charge and prove my innocence. The brokers had a scheme to keep me continuously tied up.

I knew I was locked in. Before the verdict came out, I went home, packed my things, and flew to New York to gather myself and decide what to do next.

The owner of the planing mill was a good fellow, so before I left I said to him, "Look, you take care of my things. There's a lot of money here, about $80,000 in lumber that I've paid for. Fight this out in court for me." He agreed.

It took many years of court actions until the court ordered the lumber sold to pay costs. I lost everything. I zeroed again.

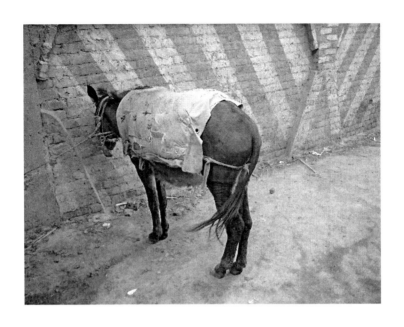

ANYTIME ONE FEELS BAD,
ONE IS NOT LOVING
ANYTIME ONE FEELS GOOD,
ONE IS LOVING

Losing businesses seemed to be a habit with me, but that didn't stop me. A week after I left Canada, I flew to San Francisco looking for lumber in Northern California. I was there for only a few weeks when I was informed that there was a good deal in New Mexico. Within a week I landed in Albuquerque.

I bought a sawmill and a planning mill for one dollar. The mills were in debt for almost $100,000, and the bank had foreclosed them. The bank sold them to me with my promise that I'd pay off the bank first, and then the labor.

I never had been in that business before. But here I was with an opportunity to get lumber, a scarce commodity, right at the source—the tree.

The sawmill was in Datil. The mill was very large, covering about half a mile alongside the railroad in Magdalena, with huge trucks, conveyors and equipment. I soon had a tremendous operation going, and I liked the bigness of it.

I started up the operation, managed to pay off all the debts—then the market for lumber collapsed! More than half of postwar business was in the hands of small saw millers like me. So the two biggest moguls had gotten together and suddenly dropped below our costs.

I had millions of board feet of board for lumber cut and drying, and owed the bank about $150,000 on it. I sold it for less than it cost me, paid the bank, and ended up with nothing.

I decided to build homes. I got a commitment for twelve homes with the Federal Housing Administration guaranteeing $100,000 of mortgages. All I needed was to own land I wanted to build on. For next to nothing I was able to get land.

I did a beautiful job on those houses, as though I were going to live in them myself. The town fathers were selling similar houses for $12,500; I was selling them for $8,000, and still making $1,500 per house.

Labor was working then at forty cents an hour. I said to the men, "I'll start you at eighty cents an hour and if you're good I'll give you a dollar. If you're not, I'll let you go." I didn't realize that I was spoiling the local low-cost labor market.

So the town fathers went for me.

They sent Leslie to get me. He had been discharged from the army as a mental case. He entered my kitchen through the back door, sat on the edge of the kitchen table and told me that I had to leave town. When I refused, he pulled out a forty-five pistol, steadied his hand on the table with fingers on the trigger and as he said, "I'm going to let you have it," my eyes focused on his trigger finger and I thought, "Is this true? Can I be killed? Maybe he'll miss or just hit me on the shoulder."

As he began to squeeze the trigger I said to myself, "This is impossible! It can't be!"

Immediately on that thought there was a sudden loud rapping on the front door. Leslie, startled, stopped his action and ordered me to go into the living room, answer the door and tell the party, "I'm busy."

I opened the door, and as I started to say, "I'm busy," my next door neighbor, not listening to me brushed me aside walked into the kitchen, exclaimed to Leslie, "What are you doing with that gun?" and took it away from him.

I never could understand what impelled him to come in the nick of time, nor could he tell me more than just, "I had a feeling to come in."

Being a strong defender of and fighter for principle I said to myself, "I'm going to throw the legal book at that guy." But then I figured, "Hell, he's got two kids and a wife." So I went to him and said, "Les, I'm forgetting about that incident." He was so relieved that he grabbed me by the hand, shaking it and exclaiming "Thank you, thank you."

Then Manuel got after me. He entered my home and said, "If you don't give me $600 for the masonry work I've done, I'm going to beat you up." The job was only worth $50.

Manuel was a big bruiser and he had another even taller and tougher friend with him. This was rough country.

I said, "You can go to hell!" The two of them started for me, and as they did, I got an idea.

I held up my hand to stop them and said, "Okay, I'll give you the money," I sat down and wrote out a check for $600.

The moment they left, I called the bank and stopped payment on the check.

Then I got into my car and drove to the bank. As I reached the entrance they were coming out. I yelled, "Ha, Ha, Ha." Right in their faces. I knew they wouldn't do anything in public.

Manuel said, "You son-of-a-bitch! I'm going to get you. You wait."

After that I thought, "If he tried it one time, he could do it again. I'd better do something." So I went up to the college of mining in the town where I knew a student who had a fast repeater pistol, a P-38, and borrowed it. From another friend I borrowed a rifle.

Later Manuel and his buddy came back. I met them outside my home and pulled the pistol on them.

"If I ever see you guys within seeing distance of this house, I'm going to kill you!" I said.

The taller one said, "Oh, you're pretty big with a gun."

I answered, "Big enough to kill you right now," as I aimed for his head and pretended I was pulling the trigger. His legs buckled but he caught himself from falling. I was under full control at the time and kept my cool.

They went away scared. They bothered me no more.

When I went into my bedroom, and saw the rifle on my bed and the pistol in my hand, I said to myself, "What the hell is going on here, Lester? Are you mad? You're *not* a gunman. What a*m* I doing?"

All this was during the time that I was on phenobarb to knock out the migraine headaches, and Dexedrine sulfate to keep me going. I had to drink every weekend to escape the so heavy world, to be able to face it again on Monday morning. I really was down, down.

Looking at the guns, I made the decision right then and there to get out. What the hell was I doing here? My friends and family were back East.

I packed up, pulled out of the area and headed East. I arrived in New York and immediately got over-busy. Not only did I start two miners working a lead mining claim in Belen, New Mexico, but at the same time raised funds and started drilling for oil in Kentucky. The workload and my anxieties culminated in a coronary thrombosis.

This extremity was the turning point in my life.

Freedom

LOVE ELIMINATES FEAR

I cut out from the world, one hundred percent. Formerly, I had been active socially in arts, opera, jazz, ballet and theater. It was my necessity for escape.

However for three months I stopped all social activity, did no dating, and even cut out the weekend visits to my sisters and their families. I also cut off the phone.

I was a total cut-out from the world. I was isolated, right in New York City. I'd go out only to buy food between 2 and 5 A.M. when the streets were emptiest.

Stores were open all night in Manhattan. I saw no one except the grocer.

I was all out, hell-bent on getting the answers.

I had spent over forty years of my life, mostly very unhappily. Friends would tell me, "Gee, Lester, you've got everything." I felt I had nothing.

I had a nice family and an unusually loving mother. I was given a good education. I was living on 116 Central Park South. My friends were many. But my life was unhappy and sick. I had suffered twenty years with hay fever, fifteen years with ulcers, half a dozen perforated ulcers, an enlarged liver and kidney stones. About twice a year I'd get jaundiced. I developed migraine headaches, then heart trouble: and fear, anxiety and frustration all my life.

After my coronary I was told I might drop dead any minute. "Don't climb stairs unless you absolutely have to, " I was warned.

That was in 1952. I was forty-three years old.

I was desperate.

This fear of dying scared me more that I've ever been scared in my life. It caused me to conclude with determination, "Either I get the answers, or *I'll* take me off this earth. No heart attack will do it!"

And I had a nice easy way to do it, too—morphine that the doctors allowed me for my kidney stone attacks.

That determination to get the answers was the thing that gave me full realization of what life and happiness are.

After a few days of fear of dying, I resolved that there was nothing I could do brooding about it.

I started thinking of a way out. I sat alone in my apartment just thinking, thinking, thinking.

I had a problem and had to get the answer. So I sat down and said, "Lester, you were considered smart. You were an honor student in high school. You won a scholarship when only three scholarships to Rutgers University were awarded through competitive, statewide examinations. You were an honor student in college." But for all of that, I was dumb! dumb! dumb! I did not know how to get the very elementary thing in life—how to be happy!

Well, what do I do?

All of my past knowledge was useless. So I decided to drop it all and start from scratch.

Okay. Well, what is this world? What is my relationship to it?

I began reviewing the little happiness I had known and it always related to a woman.

"Oh, being loved by a woman is what happiness is!" Then I thought, "Well, here I am. I've had and still have lovely women wanting me. But I am still miserable!"

I thought, "Then it is not being loved!" I began reviewing it again and I discovered that when I was loving them, I was happy.

Conclusion: my happiness equates to my capacity to love.

Then I devised a very deep process of trying to love others. I would review my past behavior. Where I thought I had been loving, I saw I wanted to be loved. For instance, when I saw that I had been nice to a girl only because I wanted something from her, I would say, "You son-of-a-gun, Lester. Correct that!" Then I would love her for what she was, not what I wanted from her. I kept correcting myself until I could find no more to correct.

The next great awareness that came to me was of what intelligence is. I got a picture of a single overall intelligence that each one of us is blindly using, available to us to the degree that we do not cut it off. Then I discovered that every thought materialized sooner or later. Therefore I took responsibility for everything that was happening to me. As I searched for it, the causal thought would come up in mind when it was conscious, I could drop it.

I was letting go and undoing the hell I had created. By squaring all love, trying to love rather then trying to be loved, taking responsibility for all that was happening to me, finding my subconscious thought and correcting it, I became freer and freer, happier and happier.

I received an interesting picture of intelligence. I suddenly got a picture of amusement park bump cars that are made difficult to steer, so that drivers continually bump into each other. They were all getting their electrical energy from the wire screen above, through a pole coming down to every car. The power above was symbolic of the overall intelligence and energy of the universe coming down the pole to me and everyone else. We were all using it and bumping into each other, instead of driving along together in harmony.

We use this intelligence in life and we just bump! bump! bump! That was the first picture I got of life and intelligence.

We all have a direct line to that infinite intelligence up there, and we are using it blindly, wrongly and against each other.

For the first two months I was getting answers to the question, "What are happiness, intelligence and love?" As the answers came I was gradually being unburdened of my miseries and tensions.

The very first insight was on love seeing that my happiness was determined by my capacity to love. That was a tremendous insight. I began to free myself. Any bit of freedom when you're plagued feels so good. I knew that I was moving in the right direction. I had gotten hold of a link of a chain, and was determined not to let go until I had the entire chain.

Then I saw that my total thinking was responsible for everything happening to me, and this gave me more freedom. I could control my life by undoing compulsive behavior, all of which had been caused in the past and was now subconscious.

The third phase was discovering and recognizing who and what I really am. I began to see that we are infinite beings with no limitations: that all limitations were only in our minds, learned in the past and retained.

When we see what we really are, we fear no limitations and can easily discard them.

Working on those three things, I became freer and freer. My heart became lighter. I was happier, more at peace. My mind got quieter. Then my curiosity took me all the way. I said, "If this is so good, I must find just how good it can get. I'll go to the limit."

I'd had a life mostly of misery. So when this wonderful happiness began, I wanted all of it. I kept at it.

And then all of a sudden powers came to me. I could know anything anywhere.

I saw there were people just like us on endless numbers of planets.

Then I took a look across the country to Los Angeles. I called up a friend and said, "In the living room there are three persons," and so on. I started telling him what was going on. Dead air! Suddenly I realized I had frightened him. I had to cut the conversation short.

I was amazed at the very pleasant sensation of watching divine laws in operation. The fascination was not in the powers themselves, but in watching and witnessing the divine law operating. I really didn't feel like a doer.

I knew that I should not latch onto these things. If I got interested in them, I'd stop progressing.

I had seen by this time that the world is nothing but a dream. To get interested in the dream through an interest in powers would lead me back into what I was trying to escape from.

Toward the end of my period of seeing, I one day saw that this whole thing is just like a dream! And it's a dream that never really was -- any more than a dream you had last night was. Was it a real thing that dream you had last night? No. It was only in your mind. But of course, until one awakens out of this everyday state, it seems real.

The new reality was that I am, and that's all there is – that my Beingness is the changeless essence of the universe. Of course I was punch-drunk, slaphappy, and in a state of euphoria.

In this state the whole world looks perfect. Looking at my body, I also saw this body as part of perfection. This instantly corrected all my ailments.

Several times on the way up I'd have a realization that would so supercharge my body, I'd have to walk for miles and miles at a good pace.

Some of those realizations are really more than a body can take. You can't sit still. Many a time I was forced to walk off the new, intense energy.

I was undoing subconscious hang-ups, tendencies, and predispositions, realizing more and more that I am free, that freedom is my basic nature. I was getting freer and freer and I automatically went into a state where, having undone enough mental limitations, my real Self began presenting itself to me.

I saw that the real "I" of me was only Beingness, was only existence, and that my Beingness was exactly the Beingness of the universe. And when I saw that, I identified with every being in this universe; I identified with every atom in it. And when you do that you lose all sense of being a separate individual, an ego.

When I saw that I AM the <u>Amness</u> of this universe, I then saw the whole world as just an image, like a dream.

I imagined or dreamt that I was a body. And I'm dreaming right now that I'm this body.

In reality, the only thing that is <u>Isness.</u> That's the real, changeless substance of everything.

And you are that, too.

When I started, I couldn't have been much lower. I was plagued with ailments accumulated over the years topped with a coronary, deep depression, and intense misery.

Three months later I was at the other extreme; I was so happy I felt I had a smile on my face that I could not take off. I felt a euphoria and lightness that are really indescribable.

Everything in life itself was open to me—the total understanding of it. It is simply that we are infinite beings, over which we have superimposed concepts of limitation. And we are smarting under these limitations that we accept as though they were real, because they are opposed to our basic nature of total freedom. But they are just mentations, mental concepts.

Life before and after was at two extremes. At first, it was extreme depression and sickness. Afterward, it was a happiness and serenity that's indescribable.

Life itself became so beautiful and harmonious that everything would fell perfectly into line. As I would drive through New York City, I would rarely hit a red light.

When I parked my car people would stop and even go into the street to help direct me to a parking space. There were times when taxicab drivers would see me looking for a parking space, and would give up theirs. And they couldn't understand why they did it. Here they were, double-parked!

Even policemen would move out and give me their parking places. And again, after they did it they couldn't understand why. But I knew they felt good, and I was always thankful to the Divine.

Everything I did in those days seemed to affect everyone around me. My vibrations made them feel good, made them feel giving, and made them more loving. And so they would try to help me.

If I went into a store, the salesman would happily go out of his way to help me. If I would ordered something in a restaurant and changed my mind, the waitress would bring just what I wanted even though I didn't tell her. Actually everyone moves to serve you as you just float around.

When you are in tune and you have a thought, every atom in the universe moves to fulfill your thought. And this is true.

Being in harmony is such delightful, delectable state, not because things are going your way, but because of the feeling of God-in-operation. It's a tremendous feeling; you just can't imagine how great it is. It is such a delight when you're in tune, in harmony—you see God everywhere! You're watching God in operation. And that is what you enjoy, rather than things, incidents, happenings. His operation is the ultimate.

When we get in tune, our capacity to love is so extreme that we love everyone with an extreme intensity, which makes living as delightful as it can be.

Life After Consciousness (A.C.)

LOVE BEARS ALL THINGS
LOVE BELIEVES ALL THINGS

I got the feeling that I wanted everyone, the rest of me, to know what I had discovered. That was the first thing that hit me. But how could I do it?

I thought I could be most effective in getting this knowledge to children through the educational system, especially to children from first grade on.

It came to me that there would be entire villages in Long Island available because of non-payment of FHA mortgages.

In the real estate business, I'd be in a position to step in. I decided to go into it. However, after I had gotten into it, it came to me that I had no right to interfere in the relationship of children with parents who wanted them to get conventional training. It would be interfering with the karma of the child and the parent. So I had let go of that plan.

Karma is the law of compensation. Everything you give out comes back to you. I had no right to interfere in what was going to be the children's way of life, because their life was going to be in accordance with choices they had made.

I realized that the only thing I should do was to present my discovery to those who wanted it.

And I knew I was going to do that.

The second thing that hit me was that I must prove everything, and being a scientist that was natural if I proved everything, I could be more effective when I talked about it.

So I went through a process of proving all this new knowledge that came to me. I began imagining things that I wanted, small things, and they came very quickly.

Then I realized that the only thing that stopped me from getting something big was that I just didn't dare to think big. So I asked myself, "What's the biggest thing I can think of in the way of things?" And I said, "Gee! A Cadillac, with a specially built body." I pictured a Cadillac with a specially built body, and I saw myself riding in it, and it was mine. Then I let go of the picture and because I was so sure I had it.

In about two weeks, an acquaintance came to me and said, "Lester I just bought you the most beautiful Cadillac," and he described it. It was the color I had in my mind, everything just as I had seen it. He said, "A friend of mine bought it, got a specially built body, but he doesn't want it, and I got it for only $4,000."

When he said that, I looked at him. I didn't have the money.

"Oh don't worry about the money," he said, "I'll pay for it."

I said to him, "Well, will you give me until tomorrow to give you my answer?"

He quizzically looked at me. Who takes a day to give an answer to a thing like that? But he said, "Yes, sure."

I thought it over. I had just gotten rid of my old car. In New York City, it was a nuisance. Also, I didn't like the idea of being ostentatious with a Cadillac. I felt a unity with people. Most people didn't have Cadillac and I did not want to be in a position that would make them envious. I also though, "Well, if I did it now, I can do it any time."

So when tomorrow came, I refused the car. It was quite a surprise and almost a shock to my friend.

And likewise, I proved every other law that I realized.

I knew from the very beginning that I would have to come back into the world. But I was so far out; I couldn't at that time.

Everybody's mind was a wide-open book. I would say to a person, if you would do this your problem would resolve. I could zero in on what they needed and I'd give it to them in one sentence. But it was too far away from them. It was of little effect.

Sometimes I would answer questions without being asked, or someone would ask me a question and my answer would be something entirely unrelated to the question. I was answering what people really wanted to know rather than the voiced question.

Then I became aware that there were groups who were studying metaphysics. What I knew couldn't be put into words—yet there were groups talking about it. I decided that I should meet the people who were talking about these things. And I was led into it.

I read all the major schools of metaphysics to acquire their language to speak to all people, only to discover that the very best language was the most simple and to-the-point everyday English.

I used to go often to Steinway Hall in New York, attending various lectures, and I met people there that I helped in small ways. But just a few individuals, that's all. I'm not a mass teacher.

To my family the change was puzzling.

My sister Doris phoned to invite me to supper. Before she could ask me, I said, "Okay, Doris, I'll be there for supper. I'll see you in fifteen minutes." And I hung up. Then I realized she hadn't even asked me!

I would visit my sister and my brother-in-law Nat, and Nat would say, "Lester, you're an engineer. Fix my radio."

I'd look at it and say, "Nat, it's just that loose tube." I'd tighten it in its socket and the set would work.

Well, after I did this six or eight times, Nat caught on and said, "Hey, Lester, there's something strange about this. Every time my radio or hi-fi goes bad, it's always just a loose tube, and you tighten it and it starts playing. How come?"

I said, "It just happens to be a loose tube, Nat." I knew he wouldn't believe me if I told him. He couldn't accept the unusual.

I just saw the radio as perfect, and only adjusted the tube to make it understandable to him.

After my realization, I wanted to prove to others that you can have anything you want. I even became a millionaire.

I started in the real estate business. My thinking was, "How many buildings can I buy in Manhattan if I have no money invested in each one?" That's what I had at the time—no money!

With no cash invested in each building, I saw that I could buy the entire island of Manhattan! I proceeded with that idea.

The first buildings I bought were two ten-family houses, contiguous as one unit. The price I got them for was so good that when the bank appraised it, the mortgage offered was more than the purchase price by a thousand dollars.

So now I had two buildings and an additional thousand dollars. Next, I put five hundred dollars down as a deposit on a contract for eighteen one-family houses in a row on East 79th Street. Within three weeks I sold the contract for a twenty thousand dollar profit.

In about two years' time, I owned twenty-three apartment houses with twenty to forty units per house. They were all bought with no cash by buying them on first and second mortgages and, if necessary, with an additional personal loan from my lawyer. The income from the buildings had to be enough to make all payments, including amortization of all mortgages, and yet show a profit.

The properties were building up a beautiful equity.

Every deal that I was in had to be good for everyone involved. That was one secret of my success.

I would go to the banks and ask if they had any real estate for sale. I discovered there were many estates that were being liquidated. When they wanted to liquidate older apartments, they wanted to do so immediately for roughly one-half of the market price. I would immediately buy them without even looking at them. I quickly sold them for three-quarters of the market price.

Things were going along beautifully. And I spent most of the time contemplating, working only four hours a day, if that much.

As I was deep in contemplation one day, I was hit with this: "Now walk out here with just the shirt on your back as Jesus did. Just walk out with nothing but that which you can carry."

I immediately stood up and walked out the door. I said, "Wait a minute, Lester. There are first mortgages, second mortgages and personal loans on these buildings. See to it that these people are taken care of first."

That decision was a mistake. I should have given it to God and everything would have been taken care of.

Well, after I got that inner direction, I unloaded the real estate at giveaway prices, except five buildings that I could not sell because they were lemons. I had bought them because I was told that they were going to be condemned in a few months by the city for a new housing project, and therefore would be profitable.

I turned those buildings over to a broker, bought a new Chrysler, and left for the West.

I wanted an isolated spot somewhere, and found this acreage I'm now on, 160 acres at a spot at the end of the road, naturally isolated from everything, a perfect retreat!

I told the broker I'd take it, even though I had no money for a deposit. In a day or two, a check came in the mail to tie it up.

I hadn't known the check was coming. It was a small check from the real estate property in New York. With it I put a down payment on this property. Shortly after, I got noticed that the city wanted those five buildings. With the money from them, I was able to close the deal and pay cash for the land.

Since 1958 when I left New York, I've been supported by letting go and letting God do it.

You see, another thing came to me when I got that direction to walk out of my New York apartment with only the shirt on my back. It was that accumulation is non-conviction. If I am to take care, I have no need to accumulate. Do birds and animals accumulate? If God takes care of them, He certainly will take care of us!

If you have full confidence you're going to be taken care of, you don't have any thought of future security. The only security there really is is to be able to produce at will.

From that day on, everything that I needed came to me, as I needed it. And it's still that way.

LOVE FLOURISHES IN LOVE

When I came to Arizona in 1958 I had no plans. I parked my body here, and remained in a state of ecstasy for approximately two years. I was alone during this time, but I was impelled from within to go out on occasion.

I went to New York to speak to small groups. Notes were taken and based on them *The Eternal Verities* was published. From that, other groups formed spontaneously.

I would talk to them for a few sessions, leave and then return in a half a year or so. They'd gather again, the same people with additional people, and again I'd hold sessions with them. The time lapse was to allow them to assimilate.

However, I quit doing this a year ago.

I really never saw myself as a teacher, and I have no wish to start anything like a new movement. People were pulling on me and I was giving because they were pulling. In the process they started taping these sessions in 1964. Because of those tapes, we now have the printed series of "Sessions with Lester."

My coming back into the world had made me see things differently. When I originally talked to groups I never saw any opposition. It was God talking to God. But now I see much opposition coming at me from people. I never saw it originally. Now I see it as my imposing when they are opposing what I'm telling them.

I feel I have no right to impose. Now I can present what I have to say in black and white and they can read it or not, as they choose. I no longer feel the need to go out. I see that most people don't want the truth. What they want is to make the world a better world. That's fine and I'm happy for them to have a better world. They're welcome to use the data that comes through me for that purpose. It is a step forward.

Most of the people seeking, I'd say ninety-five percent of them, are only seeking a good life. They're not seeking the ultimate. When they get to that place where they can make life nice and easy and comfortable, they stop their growth.

They go so high and life gets so easy—and then they level off. But what happens is that they can't remain happy. They'll never be satisfied until they go all the way. So there they are stuck. I can point out a group in

Los Angeles that I had worked closely with. Their businesses became good. The couples got along exceptionally well. Life became a ball. But now, four years later, they feel awful. Business is not as good as it used to be. They get headaches and they're very frustrated. They really are miserable.

There is no standing still. If one goes forward he is going backward. If he is going in the direction of the world he is in the opposite direction of freedom from limitation, since the world consists of limitation.

Eventually, though, everyone makes it. That's what we're all being driven toward when we're looking for happiness in the world. We're really looking for the highest and most felicitous state there is. In the world we call it happiness. But happiness isn't there, and sometimes sooner or later we leave and take the right direction.

All of my teachings are now in print. But the ones who really want what I can give are few. To quote, "Of a thousand, one seeks Me. Of a thousand who seek Me, one finds Me."

We are in a world period that is so ignorant of truth. We are so blind that we are seeking the way of the spirit via materiality. We are seeking to make an ideal materiality.

Our god today is the dollar. This country worships the dollar more than anything else. By worship, I mean we're devoted to it. You think businessmen are not devoted to money? They eat, breathe and sleep it. They really worship, but worship money. And because of it, they're unhappy; there is no peace or serenity for them.

When I first arrived in Arizona I withdrew into that beautiful high state. The only thing similar to it in your experience would be deep sleep with no dream, where you feel so good when you wake up, and you remember it.

I was in that state, but *aware*. <u>That state is awareness itself.</u> When you're in that state, any particular thing of which it is necessary to become conscious is what you do. It was definitely a withdrawal from the world. Yet, all the time, I held on to the commitments that I'm now going through. I again spoke to small groups, especially in Los Angeles and New York after two years. In 1962 I went to Phoenix, and that brought me more into contact with people. From 1965 to 1970 I was pretty active, most of the time in Los Angeles, as follows.

I bumped into an unusual scientist. His idea was to do away with poverty worldwide, by tapping the energy of the atom.

I managed a $300,000 project for him. We worked to produce aluminum metal that would have a higher thermal conductivity than silver. Silver has the highest of any know metal. This would lead to higher electric conductivity, which would lead to tapping the energy in the atom.

While in LA I became active in teaching groups. My purpose was to come more into the world. Coming back to the world is to me simply behaving as though the world is miserable and difficult as most people see it. Once you realize how effortless the highest way of life is, it takes tremendous effort to assume the opposite.

Wisdom of the "Why's"

LOVE IS CONTAGIOUS

In the beginning after my realizations, I was involved in individual healings. One thing would be healed; after that there would be another. Then it came to me that it would be far better to teach people to heal themselves.

Spiritual healing is the best; it's instantaneous. If you cannot do it spiritually, do it mentally. That's from instantaneous to quick. However, if you cannot use these two, then see a doctor. To each his own.

Spiritual healing is done by knowing the perfection that is. It causes you to let go of the imperfection by seeing only the perfection.

Mental healing is taking your mind off the sickness, and thinking of or visualizing your body as healthy. It is impossible to be sick without holding the picture of it in your mind.

I was involved with healing only a short while, and only on an individual scale. People who went along with it did have instantaneous healings, even over the telephone.

Once a girl phoned me and said, "I've been to the doctor and he said I've got a ruptured diaphragm. He wants to operate. What should I do?"

I saw her as whole and perfect and said, "Just look at it as being all perfect. You're all okay." And she said, "Yeah! That's right!" I felt her acceptance of the perfection.

I then told her, "All right, now go back to the doctor for a check up." She did, and she no longer had the rupture. The doctor was astonished.

I didn't attract any attention to myself with these healings. I was always in the background. You do not feel yourself as the healer; you must get yourself out of the way. You let go and let God. And as you do this, the healing happens.

Jesus said that it was the Father who worketh through Him. A mass teacher has to go out and talk to the masses. But he's not ostentatious about it. He feels that it is God talking to God. Jesus said that unless ye see signs, ye believe not. So He gave people signs to help them believe. All these healings are done to help someone get some spiritual revelation. Healing for the sake of healing is not really done. It has to be more than that.

In my growth I have always held in the back of my mind, that I only know that which I can do. If I say I can do something, I don't know unless I do it. This kept me from fooling myself. If I, Lester, try to perform a miracle, I cannot. If I succeed in getting Lester out of the way by letting go and letting God, then it happens. There must be no sense of doer-ship here. Radical reliance on God is what does it.

If someone tries to perform a miracle and it doesn't work for him, then his knowledge is not complete. You must have understanding. You must get your little self out of the way. You must let go and let God, and it happens immediately. But you do not think of trying it out or testing it. You know it is and you just let it be.

People ask me, "Lester, can you do miracles?" I say, "No, I can't." That's the truth. Yet there isn't anything I have not experienced by getting me, Lester, out of the way. By letting go of the sense of egoism, anything and everything can happen.

As Jesus said, "In my Father's house are many mansions." After people drop the body they go into a world similar to this where they meet old friends. The main difference is that there everything is immediate. Whatever you think comes into being right away. It is so much easier a life than this.

It's heavenly, compared to this. But because of it being so easy, there's little incentive to grow. Here, the opportunity for growth is the greatest.

If you die with an intense desire to stay with something here, you stay with it. Big executives come back to sit in their chairs and they're furious because there's another guy in there, and they can't get him out. People who want something here hang on, and they're the ghosts. Some of them are able to make a little noise like a rap on the wall, or to move blankets and small things like that. But that's as far as they can go. They can't do anything to us, though some people are frightened of them.

There is nothing in the universe that can harm us but our acceptance of the thought that we can be harmed.

***

I noticed from B. C. experience that when I had confidence, it transferred over to others. I can explain it now. Anything about which we have an absolute conviction makes it so. I was so confident I was going to get a loan from the bank! I knew it without a doubt, and that caused the banker to lean in my direction and give me a $10,000 loan without securities.

Everyone reads everyone else's mind, unconsciously. When two people meet, I smile sometimes at how they react to each other, unconsciously reading each other. I'm aware of it. We all read each other.

I was against all those things in the days before realization. I'd try to reason them out, unsuccessfully then I'd throw them out as nonsense.

I used to work seven days a week, twelve to fourteen hours a day, driven by inner anxieties. I was relieved from them by keeping myself occupied all the time. That was the main reason I worked so hard. I excused it by saying I was always starting businesses with no money, so I had to work hard. But I didn't. It was just escape.

This point should be brought out: I lived life the way a person should live it, in that I tried to be good, make money, be the best in my profession. I tried to do all the things everyone is trying to do. I was after the goals that were accepted by society—success, wealth, being known or renowned.

And I tried to do it within the rules. But I kept going down, down, down in physical and mental health, until I came to the near end with the coronary. No matter how you strive the way you're supposed to, in accordance with the rules of society and even achieving its goals, you do not get what you want. You wind up behind the eight ball. The world is actually set up that way. You can't win in the world. The world is set up to be hellish, so that we will someday transcend it and go back to being anything but a limited physical body, which is the least thing we could ever be.

I was extremely suppressed, unable to express my feelings. I became suppressed because, not understanding the world and wanting acceptance, I would suppress all my own feelings in order to have control of others. I did this from the earliest years. I became intensely suppressed, which caused me to be quite neurotic.

Carrying out the directions that the world thought right, wanting to do what they wanted, I suppressed my own feelings. I could never understand the values of the world. I was never really interested in money.

As I grew, I slept less and less until sleep disappeared entirely. We need sleep for one reason only—to escape from this world we think is so real. We want so much, but it's so heavy to us that we have to limit it to an average of eight hours a day.

When you're in tune and in harmony, you never get tired. Fatigue is due only to mental conflict. When all mental conflict is gone, you never, ever tire. All the energy in the universe is available to you when you're in tune. Should you want to use it, it's there for your use.

In the days that I didn't sleep, I had far more energy than when I did sleep. Wanting to be like other people, I started to sleep again. At first I tried it for an hour, then two hours, and finally got up to six hours. Now I keep it that way, although it still is irregular. I can sleep one hour or six. It's all the same to me now.

Before my realization, I believed the doctors and nutritionists who said I couldn't get too much protein. In the morning I'd have eggs and a big ham steak or a rasher of bacon. At noon and at the evening meal, I'd always have meat.

When I got my realization, I saw that our animal family was related to us. I looked upon them as pets. Can a man eat his pets?

If a hunger pang turns on, I turn it off, and then it's gone. So I never suffer from hunger.

This can be accomplished with practice by anyone. Do not eat when you're hungry, and eat when you're not hungry. You can still have three meals a day that way. It's just a method of mastering the body. You go into control instead of the stomach controlling you.

***

The happiest moments in my life before realization in 1952 were when I fell in love with beautiful girls. It was the same thing again and again. I'd fall madly in love, we'd eventually break apart and I'd have the insides ripped out of me.

The first time I broke up with Annette, the girl of high school and college days. It took me about five years to completely get over that. It hit me so hard that I used all my energies fighting it. I was in a constant gloom for a long time because of it. Then I met Virginia and I fell in love with her. And then we broke up. This time, it took me only three years to get over it.

Being in love was of more interest to me than anything else in life. My problem was that I was so unfree I just could not bear more of the non-freedom that I felt marriage would give me. And because I would not marry, the girls would leave me.

I didn't want to go through those agonies any more, so I had to do something about it. I knew the girls would leave me if I didn't marry them, so I evolved a system to prevent the extreme misery of parting. When a love affair reached its height, and I could see it starting to go downhill, I would begin to get ready for the break. But having suffered, I didn't want these girls to suffer the way I had. So I would have them throw me over.

I discovered that if a man chased a girl, she ran. If he ran away from her, she ran toward him. So, with words, I would start fencing them in with love. I'd say, "Honey, where have you been? You should have been here sooner. I need you around. Don't do that again." They'd get tight and uncomfortable. It was all fencing in, and I knew how to work it beautifully. This was all headwork.

I just learned by watching what made people move. I really didn't understand it psychologically.

The total effect on me of my love affairs was misery! But those blows of love, passion and then heartbreak are really good. Were it not for the blows, we'd be forever sunk in this delusion, which is bits of pleasure and long periods of pain. That's the pattern in the world – for each ounce of pleasure we pay with pounds and pounds of pain. There is so much pain that most people get accustomed to it, and don't even see the extent of it.

My first clue that a love relationship was starting to go downhill came when the girl first started hinting, then talking, and finally nagging, about marriage. When the nagging started, it was nearing the end. By that time, I would have another girl set, so that I wouldn't suffer the acute pain I had formerly suffered.

There was nothing worse that that suffering. You can't turn it off. You can't put any salve on it, except the one salve I discovered—getting another girl!

In most love relationships, that which one wants from the other is mostly ego approval. That is why the majority of people are not happily married. They're picking at each other most of the time, wanting ego approval. That makes for a bad marriage. What makes for a successful marriage? Two things—having interests in common and friendship.

I was sitting in the 23rd Street Cafeteria in New York City with two friends. This was about 1945. We were sitting around the table having pie and coffee and Joe remarked, "Gee, I never have any sex."

And I said, "Joe, what about last weekend with so-and-so?"

And Joe said, "Oh, that doesn't count."

"And what about so-and-so the weekend before that?"

"Oh, that doesn't count."

"And what about so-and-so the weekend before that?"

"Oh, that doesn't count."

Fred chimed, "Gee, I never have any sex either."

And I said, "Fred, what about last weekend with so-and-so?"

"Oh, that doesn't count."

"And what about so-and-so the weekend before that?"

"Oh, that doesn't count."

And then I got a tremendous realization. I saw that I, too, felt the same way: that I never have any sex! And I said, "Are we insane? What is this?" And I saw that what we wanted was not sex, but <u>love</u>. And not getting the love we were saying, "We're not having any sex." I let go of the feeling that I-never-have-sex after that, but it didn't help much. I still felt that I couldn't get love. I still felt that I didn't have love.

I think the reason why many people today are indulging in so much sex is that they are identifying it with love. Not finding love through it they go in for more and more sex all the time.

LOVE HAS NO PERSONAL ANGLES

You don't get free by fighting the world. You get free within.

When Nancy Sinatra was asked on a talk show what she thought of the women's liberation movement, she said she couldn't understand it. She said, "Freedom is a personal thing. I don't feel that I have to fight for freedom." She implied that she already felt she had that freedom. The whole movement made no sense to her. And she had the right idea, that freedom is a state you achieve personally.

Women are second-class citizens in our society—so much so that many of them accept it and don't even see it.

How may Presidents have been women? How many members of Congress are women? How many executives of corporations are women? The reason why women are in a secondary position is that they think of themselves as secondary. If they would correct their own thinking and actually think themselves as equal to men in everything, they would be. Then the "Women's Lib" movement would not be necessary.

The Constitution of the US has always given equal rights to all citizens—that includes women. Women who are masters do not have the acceptance that the world gives men, and therefore tend to remain out of sight.

The nature of man is reason; the nature of woman is feeling. Feeling is closer to the Self than reason. Therefore, women are closer to the Self in that they operate on feeling.

This reminds me of one businessman who never would make an important decision until he brought his client home for his wife's approval. He had learned from experience that her feelings or intuition were always right. He said he couldn't explain it, but he knew it was so.

You see, men and women are of two different natures, and this is why we have a difficult time understanding one another.

In some of the groups I've worked with, the men were brilliant and questioning. The women hardly ever said anything—but they moved beyond men! The women felt it, they experienced it. Women work by feeling; men by reasoning.

Women have the advantage.

It came to me why some men and women are homosexuals. As we go through our many, many lives, we change sex at certain times. For instance, if I had been a woman in my last lifetime, and this time I took the male body, I'd have a certain amount of natural attraction for women because of my male body, but I'd have more of my feminine feelings carried over from my last lifetime. The more lifetimes I continued in a male body, the more masculine my feelings, and the less homosexual I become. You find homosexuality among all peoples. It's natural. We change sex to get more experiences. It is good that homosexuality is more accepted today. Until recently it was criminal to be that way. That was cruel.

* * *

Infants are not mental nothingness. If you'll remember back to the days you were an infant, even to the day you were born, you'll see that you knew who your mother was, who you father was, and even who the doctor was. You knew all these things, even though you couldn't talk. You knew what was going on.

Your only interests were to satisfy your needs. If Momma didn't give you milk, you cried, and Momma gave it to you.

My oldest sister spoke at the age of six months. But I didn't talk till I was three. This caused everyone to worry about me. They though I was stupid.

But I didn't need to talk. I got everything I wanted by pointing and making a sound. I used to wonder why they were worried about me.

Not needing to talk, I didn't until I was three—but I'm making up for it now!

After my realization, I went back in memory and relieved my infancy. What every infant wants is that his needs be satisfied. If they are, he is happy; if they're not, he uses the only language he knows—crying!

A child should never be left to cry. Crying is not a lung exercise. It's a child's only form of communication. It's cruel to let a child cry without finding out what he wants and taking care of it. This taking care of the needs of children would alleviate much of their insecurity in adulthood.

Education today is total miseducation. You take an infinite being and you try to jam rote stuff into him, stifling his capacity to evolve and be creative. Do you have to teach a flower how to grow beautiful? We should have the same attitude toward a child. We should allow the child to evolve naturally, to express his inner abilities. When you look at it that way, you can see how confining our educational system is.

Take the colleges. They tell you you must learn to think for yourself. But if you think differently from the professors, you flunk.

In my first term in college, I was told, "Now that you're in college, you should think for yourself." So I started doing it. The first two marking periods I flunked all the subjects where I had to think for myself.

Not able to understand why I was flunking, I asked one of the professors if he would allow me to see the exam papers of the others who got good marks.

I read them and discovered that they were giving him back exactly what he was telling us. Then I saw the whole picture: if I thought the way he thought, I was smart; if I didn't, I was dumb, even though he told me to think for myself. So it's not true that they want you to think for yourself; they want you to think the way they think.
After that, it was easy. I kept excellent notes and made sure I always gave the Prof. his ideas. With the least amount of studying I got the best marks.

***

Progress is really not in the world, but in transcending the world. In the world we will always have misery with our pleasure. The state of ultimate well Beingness is reached only when we are totally free of worldly limitations.

***

All drugs are poisons. Poisons tend to push you out of your body and give you a feeling of detachment from its heaviness. By letting go of the attachment to the body, you expand your consciousness beyond body consciousness.

The harm in smoking marijuana or taking any drug is that you give it the credit for doing something that you can and should do without it. Being high is our natural state and must be gotten by our own doingness. The more we use marijuana or other drugs, the more we depend on them to feel high. Therefore the less capable we become of being high on our own. Also, when we do it on our horsepower rather than with drugs, we can go way beyond the limits of the highness that the drugs allow, and experience way beyond the most fantastic of our imaginings. You see, there is actually no limit to how high we can go on our own, without drugs.

One thing, however: Marijuana could be an eye-opener in that it may give you a preview of something you might never have had without it. But I don't advocate taking drugs. You can get the same preview with more intensity by just getting your mind quiet enough.

***

Cancer, close to Leo, is my astrological sign. Astrological data have been accumulated by compilations of the lives of many, many people. Therefore, they fit many people.

But my opinion is that, as those planets out there influence me, how much influence does this planet earth have on me? Earth is not considered when astrologers develop their charts. Yet, its influence is greater than all the other planets put together.

Also, who is smarter? Clods of soil out there in space, or my intelligence? The planets are matter. Should *they* determine *my* intelligence? I say, no! This is my attitude towards astrology. When matter like planets determines us, we should turn it around and determine for the planets. I'm not going to subject myself to a distant clod of dirt guiding and influencing me. Although intelligence is defined as the ability to resolve new problems, I define it as the ability to be happy. Man wants happiness more that anything else. Should not his intelligence be judged by his ability to get what he most wants?

You use your car to take you around, but you don't say, "I am the car." Like wise, your body is a carcass, or better, a "cary-case." You're using it as a vehicle now. If you say, "I am the body," it's the same as driving your car and saying, "I am the car."

LOVE IS THE MEANS AND THE END

The word "atom" by definition means the smallest indivisible particle. Up until 1952, having been trained in physics, I carefully followed the latest findings of the atom and atomic theory. The atom, which originally was supposed to have been they basic building block of the universe, already had more than thirty particles in it. I saw that it could no more be accepted as the indivisible building block.

I saw that our total knowledge of all natural phenomena added up to zero. We didn't know what gravity, magnetism, electricity, light or even heat were.

Science progresses by trial and error, because science doesn't understand natural phenomena. The reason for it is man's low understanding of the science of being. The world is on a destructive course because of that lack of understanding.

Today we get our energy by destroying matter. If you keep destroying matter, by natural principle, it's going to destroy you. And that's what's happening in the world today. An eye for an eye, a tooth for a tooth—the law of compensation!

We've poisoned the atmosphere with our destruction of fossil fuel, coal and oil. Now it's poisoning us.

We're poisoning the water. And we're poisoning the food. We can't go on doing this and survive. We must go with nature rather than destroy it. We must learn that if we continue our present direction, it will destroy us. This is already obvious. And the way is by the study of man and his Beingness, the science that would correct all other sciences because it is basic to all other sciences.

If we would let go of our destructiveness and hate, the mind would be cleared so that we could see the simplicity of nature and natural law. It is not as complicated as our physicists try to make it. Natural, infinite power is right there in front of our eyes and we can't see it. Nature is here to serve us. We're not here to fight it, smash it, or crash it. But everything we do, we do the hard way. Our basic research instrument, the cyclotron, smashes atoms.

The major science, the basic science of all sciences, the science of being, man has little or no interest in. The science of being would explain and make all other sciences. If we were in tune with nature, in tune with ourselves, loving rather than hating, nature would fulfill and serve us with bounty that would make everyone not only affluent, but also extremely happy.

All our theories keep changing. Every physicist is aware of this. If they were correct they would need no change. The atom was supposed to be the basic building block that everything else is built out of. We know that theory is wrong. And we hold on to it. Gravity and magnetism we don't understand. We don't even know what electricity is, but we can use it. Through trial and error we've learned how. By crossing a magnetic field with a copper conductor we get a current. We've learned to produce electricity that way. Why it happens, we still don't know.

We don't understand gravity—not a thing about it, why we are so earthbound. When we discover what it is, we will travel the universe freely and easily. Everything in nature goes two ways. If there's a plus, there's a minus; if there's hot, there's cold; and if there's gravity, there's anti-gravity. Only when we understand gravity will we have the key to anti-gravity. Only then can we leave this planet and travel the universe. We will travel on the magnetic lines of the universe.

While man has the destructive mind that he has now, nature keeps him bound to his planet. Otherwise he would go to other planets to conquer them. He would cause havoc, and destroy the harmony of the universe. So nature confines him here. When we get more understanding, more loving and therefore have quieter minds, we'll begin to see the natural law. Then we'll see what gravity is, and leave this planet with ease.

We'll see how to get unlimited energy from the atom, in a non-destructive way. We do know that the energy is there. We use it in our atomic bomber. As I've said before, our research into the atom is by smashing it in cyclotrons. We learn by destruction. We must reverse and learn by construction. Then we'd get the correct answers. We should look at the universe out there, and learn how it is constructing itself, and in the process the atom. Knowing how the atom is constructed is the secret to its unlimited power.

The atom of our physical universe is the photon particle. It's the smallest particle we are capable of detecting. As the light particle, it hits our retina and registers as light. That same particle is the basic force of gravity and magnetism and the energy level of the atom. But this is way-out physics, and physicists will say it is ridiculous.

Matter is nothing but energy standing at a point. Physicists know this. There is a certain amount of energy standing still in this coffee cup resting on this table. When the cup moves, it becomes energy. If I hit you with this cup, you'd know there was energy coming at you. It is really that simple.

From the highest point of view I saw that matter is frozen energy, and energy is nothing more than mind in motion – that all of it is just mentation! The whole universe is only a mentation. The whole thing is an image in our minds!

This I try to show by saying, park your mind, go to sleep. Then where is this world? Don't wake up, and it never is again! Where is that world but in your mind? Put your mind away permanently and there never again is the world.

When you see your oneness, when you see you real Self, you see the entire universe as a dream in your mind, just as in a night-dream[16].

You imagine all your dreams, characters in them, the action going on, the relationship between characters. Just as you wake up out of a night-dream, some day you wake up out of this working-state dream to the fact that you're dreaming the whole thing. You'll say, "Oh, my gosh! It's nothing but a dream!" And you'll laugh and that's the end of your being an effect of the illusion. If you come back to it, you'll try to awaken the rest of yourself.

My definition of real is: that which never changes is real. The reality is changeless. It is absolute. It is always true. Let me give you an illustration that comes from the East; you're walking along the road at dusk and there's a rope on the ground. You imagine it to be a snake. Then you get all wrought up and involved in the fear of that snake and what it can do to you.

Now the snake represents the world. The rope represents the reality. The rope is harmless, emotionless and changeless. But the snake is a terrible, dangerous thing.

The world is like that snake, an imagining, an illusion. All questions of the world are like questions about the snake. Will this snake attack me? How can I protect myself from the snake?

It's all about something that really isn't! The reality is the rope. The reality of the world is the Beingness behind it. When you get your realization, the world doesn't disappear, but your knowledge of it changes completely. Instead of the world being separate, out of

---

[16] Lester means our vision of the universe, while in the state of 'sleep', is a dream. When wake up, we lose our dream and experience real universe.

your control, you discover that it exists only because of your Beingness. You're image-ing the whole thing.

Then you see it as a dream, while before it seemed to be so real to you. That's the only difference before and after realization. But as long as you think the rope is a snake, you're very involved with it. I could give you another way, too.

The world is an illusion, just like an oasis on the desert. When you look over a desert, it sometimes looks as though there is water there. As long as you don't go over and check it, you'll always think it's water.

When you go to the spot, you discover there is no water there, only sand. The next time you look at it, you still see the illusion with this difference. Now you know it's an illusion.

When you know your real Self, you discover it's totally sufficient unto itself that you have satiety, or everything you want. And you lose your thirst for the oasis.

LOVE SEEKS ITS OWN LIKENESS

There is a natural way for each nature to achieve realization. What's natural to you is the best way for you. That's why there are four major ways that embrace everyone's nature. The four ways are the rational, which is the mental way; the scientific, which is the specific methodological way; the emotional, which is the loving and devotional way; and the active way, which is rendering selfless service to mankind.

To uncover your Self takes only wanting and longing in the right direction. When you look for the I-that-I-am, it has to be sought just behind the mind. The mind can never conceive of infinity because the mind itself is finite.

When your mind is quiet enough so that you'll see through the noise of the mind, then you'll see the real "I" that you are. The more you work to quiet the mind, the more you succeed. You keep it up until complete success is there.

Mind is only creative. What we hold in mind comes into actual manifestation. The mind thinks in pictures. If I say the word "shoe," the mind pictures a shoe, and not the word.

The mind cannot picture the words "not" and "don't". Whenever you "don't", you're holding the picture of what you don't want, and therefore you're creating that which you don't want. When I say to myself, "Don't forget your watch, Lester," I forget my watch. If I say, "Don't spill the tea," the tea spills.

It's a weird thing to watch. You'd be surprised how many negative words most people use. Check it. You'll see some interesting results. Well, for me it was natural not to use them. So when I started learning how to come back into the world I had to latch on to "don'ts". It's an established habit for me now. But remember, the mind is only creative. If you "don't" something, you're holding in mind the picture of something you do not want, but *will create*. You see, "don't" is not a picture in the mind, but the thing you are "don' ting" is. If you say, "don't fall," fall is the picture.

One can throw anything out of his mind that he really wants to. Anything you resolve to do, you do. We should think in positives. I say to people, "Give me the opposite of the negative you're thinking." And they can't do it. The difficulty is habit. But you can change a negative habit to a positive habit. Just put in a positive thought with more power than the negative habitual thought. It'll overwhelm and knock out the negative thought. One powerful thought can knock out hundreds of negative subconscious thoughts at once.

What makes the difference is the power of a thought, the amount of resolve, determination, or will power that you put behind the thought.

If you can pose and hold the question "What am I?" until what you really are presents itself, it's the fastest was to complete freedom. But I have yet to meet the person who has done it. But if you'd stay around the clock with *only* "What am I?" rejecting all other thought, in a matter of a few weeks, you'd have it. In any event, you should always have "What am I?" in the back of your mind regardless of what you're doing.

If you're not successful with that, then the next big step is to drop you ego sense. When there's no more ego, what's left over is the infinite you. If taking on the ego all at once seems too much at first, then start by dropping the effects of the ego, your tendencies, predispositions, likes and dislikes. Everyone can drop tendencies and predispositions easily, if he really wants to.

Start with the small ones and go on to bigger ones as I've told you. The simple tendency to walk on the right side of the street can be changed to walking on the left. The tendency to sleep eight hours can be changed to sleeping six.

Habitual tendencies don't have to be cut out permanently —just for a time, to demonstrate who is the master. The tendency to seek approval is a big one to deal with. Everyone's attention is taken up in seeking approval. Everyone is doing it; it's such a waste of effort and time. Let me say that when you seek, whether it's with the ultimate question "What am I?" or by dropping the ego sense or tendencies, isolation is necessary. Get quiet.

Isolation helps you quiet the mind. However, isolation can be had even in the city, or wherever you are.

I was isolated at 116 West 59th Street in the heart of New York City.

It's possible to grow every day through all our different relationships and meetings. We're here for growth, not a test. This is not a proving ground; it's a learning ground, a schoolroom. There are different grades of schoolrooms for different planets. This one is a postgraduate course. It is one of the most difficult, and therefore affords the greatest growth. All of us who are here are advanced souls—advanced in that we have chosen an extremely difficult place of abode. We wanted a higher course, a tougher one, and we got it!

***

The vast majority of people's concepts of love are only concepts. "I need you, I must have you, I can't live without you, you're mine," are all non-love. Love is letting the other one have what the other wants, not what *I* want. What we call love in this world is usually a sensual, selfish emotion. Sex and love are often thought to be the same, and they're not. If you want to know what sex is, observe animals. Sex is a means of procreation. If we were living normal sex lives, we'd use sex only for that purpose. Man superimposes love on sex.

Fortunately and unfortunately, sex brings us closest to God. It usually brings out the finest of our feelings. It is fortunate in that we begin to get a taste of our feelings of love, and unfortunate in that it pegs us there and prevents us from getting deeper and more intense feelings of love. Unknown to most is that when our love is capable of being expressed directly and not limited to the senses, it has no limits and therefore our joy has no limits. Joys can be and should be thousands of times greater than the greatest joy we have ever experienced in sex.

I would suggest two things: First, to know the foregoing. Second, moderation, or even restraint, if possible, until one constantly has more joy than sex can give. Then it is easy to let go of it because you don't want to be limited in your joy. You want to keep on increasing it until you reach the ultimate joy.

An illiterate person has a much better chance of achieving total freedom because he's not clogged by accrued, accumulated encrustations of dogma, doctrine, education, ideas. The fewer ideas we have, the less education we have, the less demand we have to behave in accordance with the world, and therefore we're freer to dive into ourselves. The less we accept from society, the less cobwebs we have because society is very much in the wrong direction. So anything it gives us becomes an obstacle.

The start of the feelings of failure comes from the earliest days. Our parents tell us what to do and what no to do. Every time we want to do something and they say, "Don't", we feel we can't, we don't know how. If we don't want to do something and they say, "do," again we feel that we don't know. All the "doing" and "don'ting" by parents give us the feeling that we can't, we don't know, from the first days on. And this continues because it goes on through everyone's life.

All teachers have it as part of their make-up that we cannot do. So they tell us what to do, and repeat it, and pound it into us, and they continue that negativity that started at infancy.

So maybe ninety-nine percent of us have a feeling of failure that we can't *do*. We don't know how.

When we look at ourselves as we really are, and discover what we are, we discover that all things are possible to us, that all intelligence is available to us, that we have a direct line to omniscience, to omnipotence. And the only thing that keeps us from using it is these preindoctrinated dictums from our parents and teachers: Do. Don't.

So, by discovering ourselves we see how ridiculous it is to hold to the concept that we cannot. And we see that everything is possible; methodically that concept is dropped.

There should be no negative words in any language – no "can'ts" no "don'ts" no "not's". Really it would be terrific thing if we took them out of our language. You'll discover that you can say everything you want to say in a positive way. *Think only what you want, and that is all that you will get.*

All in all, it's the inabilities pounded into us from birth on that limit us. Our parents have it: their parents gave it to them. It goes on and on and on, unconsciously being handed down to those whom we think we love so much.

LOVE IS A FREEING OF THE OTHER ONE

I've experienced everything that I talk about; that's why it's effective when I talk to others. If I read it in a book, it would have no import to the ones I'm speaking to. But when one experiences it and then tells it, infinite power is right behind it. There is a power in his word, even when it is written down after it is said.

But it is felt even more so when it is person to person. Man is really infinite, and considers himself the opposite. Just quiet your mind enough and discover that which is just behind your mind – your omniscience. Wherever you are, you can use every incident, every relationship to grow by. Just don't stop seeking. Seeking should be a twenty-four hour quest. Almost everything you're doing is unfree behavior. Examine it and let go of it. Every time you see non-love, turn it to love. Only when you are all-loving are you free.

Get to the place where no one and nothing can disturb you. Take full responsibility for what's happening to you. Get the habit of bringing the unconscious causative thought up into consciousness, so that you can drop it and be free of it.

I developed this. Every time anything unpleasant happened to me, I would say, "What did I do to cause this?" Immediately the causative thought would come up, and I would see it and drop it.

I was driving to Los Angeles with Bill Cass. We had been driving all day and night, and I was tired. We were nearing San Bernardino. Bill said, "Lester, do your eyes hurt you?" I was tired so I didn't even answer, but I was listening to him. Then the radio announced high smog in that area. And a second time Bill asked, "Lester, are your eyes smarting?" Again, being very tired, I didn't answer. However, his thought went into me, subconsciously.

The next day my eyes were burning and tearing. As I lay back with closed eyes on the bed in a Los Angeles motel, I asked myself, "Now what did I do to cause this?" Then I heard Bill saying it the first time. I reversed it. Then I heard the radio saying it. I reversed that. And I heard Bill saying it the second time and again I reversed it. I opened my eyes and there was no more burning, no tearing. And that was the end of it!

You have to reverse everything you hear that's negative; otherwise it goes in subconsciously. You reverse it by dropping the negative and then asserting the positive. "My eyes are fine, my eyes are perfect." If, when Bill had asked me whether my eyes were smarting,

I had answered, "My eyes are fine," everything would've been okay then. I would not have accepted subconsciously that smog causes my eyes to smart and tear.

Always reverse the negatives that you hear, *each time as you hear them*. We live in a time when there is so much negative emphasis all around us, that it's necessary to do this, if we want a good, happy life. Because of so much negativity in the world, it's so difficult to get quiet. You really have to isolate yourself in New York City. Isolation from the world is dogged determination to avoid the outer worldly direction and dive deeply into the inner direction of seeking your real Self, so much so that you keep your direction and attention constantly inward.

One day we'll all wake up to the dream, see that it was a dream, and laugh at the whole thing. Meanwhile, in the dream I'm trying to wake the others out of it, if they want to wake up. I feel no urgency. But for those who want it, for the rest of me who wants this, now the teaching is available. I would gladly give them my hand and pull them up to awareness if they would go to it, if they would take the direction and work at it as a daily routine – continuing to grow by getting freer and freer every day, until they're totally free.

People don't get discouraged. Life gets easier for them; the initiative drops away. The original incentive was to get out of the misery of life. When they get that far, the goodness of it is not enough incentive for them, so they stop and level off. It's because subconsciously they want to hold on to the worldly bodies, and they feel they'll lose them if they go all the way.

You have to die to the body. Jesus did. But that does not mean dropping the body. It means dropping all the attachment to it. If you want to know how attached you are to the body, just imagine—but don't do it—throwing your body off a cliff or in front of an automobile. You wouldn't hesitate to throw an old overcoat in front of an automobile, would you? Because you are not attached to that old overcoat.

But you cannot transcend the body by killing it. If you kill the body before you're able to consciously walk out of it, you'll only have to get a new body, be reborn again, and wait twenty years or so before you can start on the path again—all a terrible waste of time!

You transcend the body when you can consciously exit it. Then you never have to return to the extreme limitation of the physical body. You'll either go all the way back Home, or move into the much higher heavenly realms. But you can never transcend it until you consciously walk out of it.

It's easy—or it's impossible.

You can start by breaking habits of the body. Start with the easy ones, like shaving first on the side of your face you normally shave last. Put on your clothes and take them off in a different order from the usual. Be conscious of the fact that you're doing something habitually, then change it.

You can change habits. I emphasize, never suffer when you do these things. Do that which you can do. If you do the little things, you can eventually do the big ones.

The way I got quite a number of people to let go of smoking was to say, "Look at that cigarette. Ask who's the boss! The inanimate cigarette or you?" If you make a firm decision that you are the boss, you throw the cigarettes away, and they never bother you again. In these ways you come to know that habits of the body do not run you, and you re-establish your mastery over your body. This leads you to seeing that the body is merely your puppet—and not you!

LOVE IS ACCEPTANCE

People who surrender to Jesus get an experience, which is delightful, wonderful. It feels right. Associated with it are love and good feelings. These should be expanded.

However, people having complete methodology cannot continue their growth.

Growth must be continuous until the ultimate is achieved. It must be daily. If we are not going forward, we are necessarily going backward. Sustained growth is absolutely necessary if we want to achieve the goal. And for this we must know the complete way. I think this thought might be an aid to those who are so uplifted by Jesus: don't believe in Jesus, but believe as Jesus believed. Emulate Jesus.

Behave as Jesus behaved.

Also, the highest point of His way was the Resurrection, the attaining of immortality; the Crucifixion was only a step to the Resurrection. Seek to attain what he attained —immortality!

Orthodox religions are good in that they teach God and good. I go farther. I try to teach from the top. I say, God is all and God is perfect. If God is all, that certainly must include us. Orthodox religions are led by too many people who don't have the realization or revelation of this perfection.

Preachers should tell people what great, infinite beings they are, made in the image of God—not that they are lowly sinners. It's terribly destructive to man to tell him he's no good, when in truth he's just the opposite! He's infinitely good in his basic nature, and this ought to be brought out.

Since God is all, our basic Beingness is God, and goodness and love are our inherent nature.

Yet any religion is ahead of all other studies because it speaks of God and good. Science speaks of the machine as God. Materiality speaks of money and fame as God. Religion is ahead of psychology, philosophy and the like, because it's in a more correct direction.

Beginning with "Genesis," the Bible is the story of our descent as God into gods, and then into man. "Revelation" is just the reverse; it tells of the seven states that man goes through to return to his God-state.

The Bible was originally very good, very high and inspiring, with specific methodology, as it should be. But because so many people without full understanding retranslated it, most of the methodology has been left out.

Where is the methodology in the Bible? That's the most important thing: How to do it!

Our Bible is also codified. The Book of "Revelation" is a code based on inspirational revelation. Even ministers who have spent their lives studying it cannot understand "Revelation," the most important chapter of the Bible.

I've always advised people to get the Red Letter Edition of The New Testament, and read only the red letters. The Red Letter Edition has everything said by Jesus printed in red—the rest in black. There you have set out the very best of the Bible, the direct words of Jesus.

Jesus came only to show us the way back to our Godhead. He came to show us the way to our immortality and limitlessness, and He taught those things that would get us there.

He said, "Greater things than these, ye shall do," implying that we shall do things even greater than those He was doing. He set an example for us to follow. But the example was for us to follow in His footsteps, and to do what He did, and through that be what He is. This is true if you surrender to Jesus. Surrender cannot be lip service. Surrender to Jesus means carrying out His will and His way, which amounts to living as a Christ!

I knew there were men before me who had discovered this like Jesus, and they are still around.

They do exist in a body, one made of finer substance than our body. They are still with the world, helping those of us who want help. Being in the higher realm, they are far more helpful because they can be anywhere at any moment.

They are conscious of the fact that separateness is a dream. They are conscious of their commitment to help those in the dream wake up out of the dream - and know that they too, are the infinite One.

There is never a time when these great ones are not offering their hands. It's called grace. It's gotten by one way only—through surrender. Not my will, but Thy will be done. It's pushing the ego sense to the background, and letting it go, for the time being. That allows Them in.

The thing that allows us to surrender is the desire to surrender. It's simple. When we really desire to surrender, we do it. But the desire to be this big-shot ego-body is so strong with us that we don't easily let go of it. It is usually stronger than the desire to let in the great ones.

If you can surrender, you can meet with Jesus.

Every meeting you have with these great ones leaves you other than what you were before. They always do something for you. They leave you with a tremendous new revelation. They never leave you the same. And this is the way you can tell whether the meeting is real, or whether it's just your imagination.

It's difficult, because a great one usually is humble and his qualities are inner qualities. Of the things to look for, I would say the greatest is a teacher's inner, imperturbable peace. He does not go up on praise, nor down on condemnation. Next, he sees everything with equal mindedness. Everyone is treated alike by him. He shows not one ounce of favoritism toward anyone, whether that one is an angel, a devil, or an animal.

Contentedness and complete acceptance of all that is, are also signs to look for. Lastly, he gives his knowledge freely.

A Master is one who has become a master over his body and a master over his mind, and thus has achieved the ultimate freedom. The world "guru" means teacher. With a capitalized "G" it means a fully realized teacher, or a Master.

A Master can help us go free.

Could you imagine the ocean to be infinity? Well we, the ocean of Beingness, imagine little tiny circles around parts of us that we call drops; and this drop says, "I am separate from that drop and separate from all the other drops." It's an imagined circle around part of the ocean calling itself a drop. But actually, every drop is the ocean. It has all the qualities of the ocean: it's wet, it's salty, it's H2O, and so forth. And everything that the infinity is, we are. When you see the truth, only then do you understand this.

All the masters never lose sight of the oneness or allness. But they choose to play-act a game of separateness, to help the rest of their Self that's asleep to wake up out of the dream of separateness. It's that simple. Your point of view changes when you get realization from separateness to oneness. Simple! Simple! Simple!

Before, everything is separate from you. After, everything is in you. Before, the world seems intensely real. After, you'll see the panorama of life as a dream. You'll know it's dream texture and you'll let the dream run. Then, when you're ready to leave the dream, you gather in all your forces, and with a big smile on your face, you consciously exit the body into your immortality.

The real you is your very own real Self, the "I" of you as you really are. It is not confined to the body or mind that you now think you are. Our real Beingness, our real Self, is like the screen in a cinema show. Your real Self is the changeless screen and the flitting pictures are the world.

The Self of us, the screen, never moves, but all the pictures on the screen do. When you're looking at characters on the screen and all the play that goes on, the fires, floods, and bombs don't touch the screen. The fires don't burn it; the floods don't wet it; the bombs don't destroy it.

That screen, like our very own Self, is changeless and untouchable.

But superimposed on the Self as on the screen is all this action. When you wake up to the fact that this is a cinema show, from that point on you know world action to be as real as the movies.

My wish for everyone is that everyone attain the highest state possible, so that here on earth we have that heaven that everyone dreams of, where life is beautiful, life is easy, and everyone has the greatest love and respect for everyone else. This would cause all misery to drop away, all sickness to disappear, all thoughts of war and destructiveness to be eliminated from our minds, and in place of it, just the opposite: love, beauty, and joy.

To sum up, my overall wish is for everyone (the rest of me) to fully know what I know, so that all misery and unhappiness may end.

Recorded in Arizona, 1972

The Supremacy of Love

There is love and there is true Love. Small love is often passionate and blinding, it is usually short lived; it is not accepting (or it is accepting only something about another person); it is selfish, always expecting something in return; it is enslaving: you are mine! Love to a man or a woman is usually like that, which is why it often ends in disappointment. Exceptions do exist, but they are rare (see chapter *Partner for Life* in *Book Two*). More often this love ends either in divorce or in compromise that inevitably leads to something like 'nothing is worse than loneliness together'. Even love to a child is limited. It is conditioned by possessiveness, domination, lack of total acceptance, and it always wants the child to love back. Though every kind of human love has roots in total Love, which everyone harbors within, this little love can never make one perfectly happy.

We have the ability, right in this moment, to connect with the wonderful, amazing energy of Love, the most powerful energy in the universe.

True Love is acceptance that knows no exceptions; it is understanding and compassion. It is serene and intense, but not possessive; it doesn't expect anything in return. Love includes all human values.

It is obvious that in order to begin moving towards true or total Love, first we need to love ourselves unconditionally. If we don't feel good about the person in the mirror, no one outside will give us what we are lacking. Identifying with the Love that is within immediately makes us to feel better. When we love ourselves, we are calmer, happier, confident and more secure. When loving, we are considerate and much gentler in the way we approach people and situations. Each time we release, we are moving into harmony and into the power of Love.

Love is sharing. In the past, I've organized several Russian-American Investment Symposiums at Harvard University. There were eleven Russian associates in my Moscow office. Some year I made over $250.000 in profit. Over several years, I could make over one million dollars, since it was my business, and all my employees were on salary. However, I decided to share all profits with employees. This decision was only possible with Love.

In their higher expression Love and Awareness are one and the same. Moving in the direction of Love and Awareness – coming home – will dramatically alter life in a positive way. We all know that to change one's self is the most difficult task. However, we don't really need to change anything: our capacity and intensity to love are the only qualities we need to open in ourselves in order to become Love. Everything else within ourselves and in our world will then adjust itself accordingly, including attitudes of people we have relationships with. Love is a mystery that moves worlds and transforms lives. When our Love is total we are perfectly happy.

- If I speak in the tongues of humans and angels but have no love, I have become a reverberating gong or a clashing cymbal.
- If I have the gift of prophecy and can understand all secrets and every form of knowledge, and if I have absolute faith so as to move mountains but have no love, I am nothing.
- Even if I give away all that I have and surrender my

body so that I may boast but have no love, I get nothing out of it.

- Love is always patient.
- Love is always kind.
- Love is never envious or vaunted up with pride. Nor is she conceited, and never is she rude.
- Never does Love think of self or ever get annoyed.
- Love never is resentful, never glad with sin, but always glad to side with truth.
-Love bears up under everything, believes the best in all, there is no limit to her hope, and never will she fall.
- Love never fails. Now if there are prophecies, they will be done away with. If there are tongues, they will cease. If there is knowledge, it will be done away with.
- Right now three things remain: faith, hope, and love. But the greatest of these is love.

St. Paul in I Corinthians, 13

Bibliography

Asvaghosa, *The Awakening of Faith*, Dover   Publications, Inc, New York, 2003

Blavatskaya, Elena, *Voice of Silence*, Sfera, Moscow, Russia, 1999

Blavatskaya, Elena, *Secret Doctrine*, Eskimo-Press,Moscow, Russia, 2000

Blofeld, John, *Zen Teaching of Huang Po*, Grove Press, New York, 1959

Buddha, *The Diamond Sutra*, Shambhala, Boston, 1985

Cleary, Thomas, *The Taoist I Ching*, Shambhala, Boston, 2000

Evans-Wentz, W. Y., *The Liberation*, Oxford, University Press, London, 1979

Fadiman, James & Frager, Robert, *Essential Sufism*, HarperSanFrancisco, 1997

Hartong, Leo *Awakening to the Dream*, Non-Duality Press, Salisbury, United Kingdom, 2001

Lao Tsu, *Tao Te Ching*, Vintage Books, 1972

Levenson, Lester, *The Final Step to Freedom*, Lawrence Crane Enterprises, Sherman Oaks, CA, 2001

Lloyd, Virginia, *Choose Freedom*, Freedom Publications, Phoenix, Arizona, 1983

Price, A. & Wong Mou-Lam, *The Sutra of Hui Neng*, Hyperion Press, Inc., Westport, Connecticut, 1973

Rajnish, Bhagavat Sri, *Tantra* and other discourses, Osho International Foundation, 1973, Rajneesh India Poona, 1984

Red Pine, translator, *Zen Teaching of Bodhidharma*, North Point Press, San Francisco,1989

Vivekananda, Swami, *The Yoga and Other Works*, Ramakrishna-Vivekananda Center, New York, 1996

Wood, Ernest, *Zen Dictionary*, Charles E Tuttle Company, Tokyo, Japan, 1988

Yogananda, Paramahansa, *Autobiography of a Yogi*, Self-Realization Fellowship, Los Angeles, 1987

About the author of *Freedom Technique*

Yuri Spilny was born in Vladivostok, Russia. His life has in many ways been varied and unusual. In 1960, after six years in Naval Academy he decided it was not for him. "While awakening for a duty, I was hit with this," he says: "Now walk out of here!" And I left the Academy just three months before graduation." He went to Moscow Film School, and began a successful career of a documentary filmmaker. He arrived in North America in 1973 and devoted himself to the study of comparative religious philosophy, the practice of meditation, Yoga and Releasing. Traveling the world, he produced over 70 documentary films on a wide variety of subjects, including *Great Siberian Adventure, Seal Hunters* and *Inside the KGB*. He lectured at the University of Economics and Moscow State University on *Awareness, Responsibility, Releasing,* and *Freedom*. He lectured at UCLA for the Ivy League Association of Southern California on *The Psychology of Doing Business in Eastern Europe*. He also wrote *The Incredible Adventures of Kitto*. "I always knew," he says, "that my destiny was to write." Beautifully illustrated by Anna and Nadezhda Balzhak with more than eighty original watercolors, this trilogy of fairy tales emphasizes to young readers that "every child is born to succeed." His most recent book was a novel *Gates of the Dead...* a flight from grief in search of happiness; an enlightening adventure, a quest for a dream.

Yuri lives in Sequoia National Forest, California.

yuri@bookstoenjoy.com

CPSIA information can be obtained at www.ICGtesting.com
Printed in the USA
LVOW071528141112

307325LV00011B/2/P